IMAGES OF

UNITED STATES MILITARY HELICOPTERS

RARE PHOTOGRAPHS FROM WARTIME ARCHIVES

Michael Green

Pen & Sword
AVIATION

First published in Great Britain in 2017 by
PEN & SWORD AVIATION
An imprint of
Pen & Sword Books Ltd
47 Church Street
Barnsley
South Yorkshire
S70 2AS

ISBN 978-1-47389-484-6

A CIP catalogue record for this book is available from the British Library.

Typeset by Concept, Huddersfield, West Yorkshire HD4 5JL.
Printed and bound in India by Replika Press Pvt. Ltd.

Pen & Sword Books Ltd incorporates the imprints of Pen & Sword Archaeology, Atlas, Aviation, Battleground, Discovery, Family History, History, Maritime, Military, Naval, Politics, Railways, Select, Social History, Transport, True Crime, and Claymore Press, Frontline Books, Leo Cooper, Praetorian Press, Remember When, Seaforth Publishing and Wharncliffe.

For a complete list of Pen & Sword titles please contact
PEN & SWORD BOOKS LIMITED
47 Church Street, Barnsley, South Yorkshire S70 2AS, England
E-mail: enquiries@pen-and-sword.co.uk
Website: www.pen-and-sword.co.uk

Contents

Dedication

The author is dedicating this work to US Marine Corps Lieutenant Colonel Armond H. DeLalio, recipient of the Navy Cross for heroism as pilot with Marine Scout-Bomber Squadron 241 during the Battle of Midway in June 1942. He was also the first Marine certified as a helicopter pilot on 8 August 1946 and commander of the US Navy's first helicopter squadron, VX-3. Lieutenant Colonel DeLalio was killed during a helicopter test-flight accident in 1952.

Introduction

This book covers in broad detail the American military's long involvement with helicopters that began during the Second World War and continues into the twenty-first century. Reflecting their limited design capabilities, from the 1940s into the 1950s the early piston-engine-powered helicopters were unarmed as they lacked the lifting power to carry weapons. They did, however, prove their worth in both the Second World War and the Korean War in the medical evacuation role.

By the time the American military became involved in the Vietnam War, experiments had already demonstrated the potential of weapon-armed helicopters. The main limiting factor remained the relatively low lifting capacity of reciprocating-engine-powered helicopters. A focused study by industry and the armed forces paved a path to the successful marriage of advanced relatively lighter airframes, light yet powerful armaments and gas turbine engines capable of mating all those elements together in a rotary wing platform.

As successive generations of ever more powerful gas turbine engine-powered helicopters have entered the American military inventory, they have demonstrated that they have become more capable than their predecessors. Equipped with the latest in avionics, they can fly around the clock in almost any type of weather down to tree-top level to deliver personnel or destroy with guns, rockets and missiles any identified enemy threat.

The relatively recent introduction of tilt-rotor aircraft into the American military arsenal in place of existing helicopters will also be examined in this book. Combining into a single platform the useful aspects of fixed-wing and rotary-wing aircraft, tilt-rotor aircraft may someday replace traditional American military helicopters.

Acknowledgments

The bulk of the non-copyrighted images in this work belong to the various armed services that make up the United States Department of Defense (DOD) and their respective website photograph archives. Thanks must also be given to Piasecki, Bell and Sikorsky for selected images.

Some contemporary pictures of current and preserved historical American military helicopters were supplied by friends named in the photo credits. As always, Paul and Loren Hannah were most generous in sharing their photographs with the author. As with all published works, authors also depend on friends for assistance in reviewing their work and in this case Pete Shyvers was especially helpful.

Notes to the Reader

1. The chapter headings are the author's attempt to divide the history of American military helicopters into manageable portions. With that said, many of the helicopters featured in this work transcend the author's chapter headings, reflecting the multi-purpose nature of many helicopters.
2. The official designation codes applied to American military helicopters are seldom employed except in official documents. Many helicopters have been assigned official nicknames, with others having acquired unofficial nicknames that reflect some design feature or combination of their letter prefix designations. In some cases the unofficial nicknames are better known than the official nicknames.
3. The listed operational parameters of the helicopters discussed in this work such as top speed, range, service ceiling and maximum loaded weight are theoretical. Weather, altitude and outside air temperature can dramatically affect the operational parameters of helicopters as well as the amount of weight they can carry on any given flight.
4. As some helicopter models are upgraded during their time in service, they may be fitted with external features from newer versions. This can sometimes make precise identification of a specific helicopter difficult without access to their individual data plates.

Chapter One

Piston-Engine Helicopters

America's first production military helicopter was designated the R-4B by the US Army Air Forces (USAAF) in 1944. It was designed and built by the Sikorsky Aircraft Company, with the pilot and a passenger sitting side-by-side. The fuselage consisted of metal tubing covered by fabric. The prototype of the R-4B flew in January 1942, with pre-production units being ordered for testing early the next year.

The prefix 'R' in R-4B according to the USAAF wartime aircraft designation system stood for a rotary-wing aircraft. The number '4' in the designation represented the builder production sequence for the aircraft. The 'B' was to distinguish a minor model difference. In US Coast Guard service the R-4B was labelled the HNS-1.

The US Navy had assigned helicopter development to the US Coast Guard in early 1943. The US Coast Guard serves at the direction of the US Navy during wartime. As a result of the US Coast Guard's pioneering work with the helicopter during the Second World War, the US Navy took over its development following the end of the conflict.

The piston-powered (reciprocating) engine on the R-4B produced 185hp. Of the 100 R-4Bs built (including pre-production test units) during the Second World War the American military took approximately half, with the other half going to the British military via Lend-Lease. In British military service the helicopter was named the 'Hoverfly'. Most went to the British Royal Navy.

Wartime Usage

During the Second World War the R-4Bs were employed by the USAAF in different roles. This included, for example, moving small aircraft components between supply vessels and air bases. The R-4B also performed the casualty evacuation (CASEVAC) role, although no medical care was provided by the helicopter crew. A USAAF R-4B executed the first combat search and rescue (CSAR) mission in Burma in April 1944, saving four Allied soldiers trapped behind enemy lines. Non-combat rescue missions are described as Search and Rescue (SAR).

The US Coast Guard was convinced early on of the helicopter's potential as an anti-submarine warfare (ASW) platform. By 1944, a handful could be found on Coast

Guard cutters involved with convoy protection duties in the mid-Atlantic. Their assigned mission was to identify the location of enemy submarines for dedicated ASW surface ships to engage. The R-4B lacked the payload capacity to carry any ASW weapons.

Progressively-Improved Models Appear

A follow-on version of the R-4B for the USAAF had an all-metal streamlined fuselage and was fitted with a more powerful piston engine that produced 240hp. It was assigned the designation R-6A and entered service in early 1944. It was designed by Sikorsky but out-sourced and constructed by Nash-Kelvinator. This was typical of wartime production, as some or all of a design was contracted to third parties to increase overall output.

In US Coast Guard wartime service and in early post-war US Navy use, the R-6A was designated the HOS-1, which translates to helicopter/observation/Sikorsky model one. In total, 225 units of the two-man R-6A were built. As in the R-4B, the pilot and a passenger sat side-by-side.

Larger than the R-4B and R-6A, and more capable, was the two-man Sikorsky R-5A. Unlike the R-4B and the R-6A, the pilot and a passenger sat one behind the other (in tandem). The prototype had flown in August 1943 and impressed the USAAF sufficiently for it to order twenty-three pre-production trial units in early 1944 designated the YR-5A.

Testing of the pre-production YR-5A units began in March 1945 and went well enough for the USAAF to place an order for 100 production units designated the R-5A. This CSAR helicopter was powered by a piston engine that produced 450hp.

A Must-Have Helicopter

Even as the R-5A and a modified version labelled the R-5D were entering post-war American military service, the USAAF decided that a larger post-war version of the same helicopter, designated the S-51, was a better choice. The result was the cancellation of the R-5 series with only thirty-four being completed and placement of an order for 100 units of the new S-51.

The S-51 had room for a pilot in the front of the fuselage and three passengers on a bench seat behind the pilot. Like the R-5 series, S-51s acquired by the USAAF were powered by a single piston engine. In USAF service the S-51 became the R-5F.

With the formation of the United States Air Force (USAF) in 1947, a new aircraft designation system appeared in the following year. The letter prefix 'H' for helicopter replaced the earlier prefix letter 'R' for rotary-wing aircraft. The S-51 therefore became the H-5F.

A CSAR/SAR version of the S-51 that appeared in service with the USAF in 1948 was designated the H-5G. Another USAF model fitted with an arrangement of wheels and floats was assigned the designation H-5H. The letter suffix following the number represented a sequence of minor changes to the helicopter's design.

S-51 in US Navy Service

In US Navy service the first two examples of the S-51 tested were designated the HO2S-1 with the remaining eighty-eight units labelled the HO3S-1. During the Korean War these performed in the CASEVAC and CSAR roles. These also directed the fire of US Navy warships on enemy coastal positions. In some situations the helicopter was used to identify the location of enemy sea mines.

The best-known mission of the US Navy's inventory of HO3S-1 helicopters during the Korean War was the CSAR role. This was portrayed in the 1954 Hollywood movie *The Bridges at Toko-Ri* starring famous American actors of the day such as William Holden, Mickey Rooney, Fredric March and Grace Kelly.

S-51 in USMC Service

Those US Navy S-51s provided to the US Marine Corps (USMC) were also designated the HO3S-1. During the Korean War (1950–53) the helicopter performed the following roles: CASEVAC, CSAR, reconnaissance, liaison, and command and control. When a helicopter flight crew member provided medical care to a wounded passenger, it became a flying ambulance referred to as a MEDEVAC.

One innovative use of the HO3S-1 by the USMC during the Korean War was in laying communication wire over the country's many mountains while at times under enemy fire. Without helicopters this may have been impossible.

Original Helicopter Designations

Early post-war US Navy helicopters were assigned a mixed letter and number designation. As already mentioned, the initial prefix letter 'H' stood for helicopter. Experimental helicopters had the letter 'X' placed in front of the letter 'H'. Pre-production helicopters intended for testing had the letter 'Y' in front of the letter 'H'.

The second letter in a production helicopter's designation indicated its primary role, such as 'O' for observation, 'R' for transport, 'T' for trainer and 'U' for utility. The number following the prefix letters in the designation represented the sequence in which the helicopter was built by the manufacturer. The next letter identified the builder, such as 'S' for Sikorsky. However, not all builder identification code letters began with the first letter of the firm's name.

Following the manufacturer's identification code letter there was a hyphen and a number. This number represented a sequential modification to the helicopter identified. Hence, HO3S-1 was an observation helicopter, the third built by the manufacturer Sikorsky, with one or more significant design modifications.

A USMC general in a memorandum to the Chief of Naval Operation (Air) during the early part of the Korean War wrote the following:

> There are no superlatives adequate to describe the general reaction to the helicopter. Almost any individual questioned could offer some personal story to emphasize the valuable part played by [the] HO3S ... There is no doubt the enthusiasm voiced ... is entirely warranted ... No effort should be spared to get helicopters – larger than the HO3S if possible – to the theater at once, and on a priority higher than any other weapon. We [need] helicopters, more helicopters, and more helicopters.

The HO3S-1 did have some design deficiencies that hindered its combat usefulness. The tricycle landing gear and the helicopter's high centre of gravity made it unstable when landing on anything other than a flat hard surface. The location of the engine on the top of the fuselage made it difficult to maintain in the field. Despite these design issues and more, it is a measure of its usefulness that these shortcomings were tolerated.

USMC HO3S-1 Replacements

As a replacement for the HO3S-1 during the Korean War, the USMC took into service forty-eight units of the four-man Sikorsky HO5S, beginning in 1952. It was based on the earlier Sikorsky S-52 helicopter design that was not adopted by any of the other services, although the US Army had tested four prototypes. The HO5S had a piston-powered engine that produced 245hp and was the first American military helicopter with all-metal rotors.

Unlike the tricycle landing gear of the HO3S-1, the single piston-engine-powered HO5S had a quadricycle-landing gear with self-centring front wheels. Stretcher-borne passengers were loaded through the hinged front-end cabin into the enclosed metal fuselage. Design flaws uncovered by the USMC employment of the HO5S during the Korean War led to its replacement.

The Kaman Helicopter

The USMC post-Korean War replacement for the Sikorsky HO5S proved to be eighty-one units of a military version of the Kaman Aircraft K-600. Rather than having a single rotor, the helicopter had two intermeshed rotors located side-by-side on separate pylons, earning it the unofficial nickname of the 'Eggbeater'.

In USMC service the Kaman K-600 was designated the HOK-1, which translates to helicopter/observation/Kaman number one. It could also perform the CSAR/SAR and CASEVAC roles if required. It could carry four people: pilot, co-pilot and two passengers. Empty, the HOK-1 weighed 4,334lb and had a maximum take-off weight of 5,995lb.

By the early 1960s, as the American military involvement in the Vietnam War began, it was clear to the USMC that the thirty-five remaining units of the HOK-1 in its inventory were obsolete and something new was required. None would be sent to South-East Asia and all were soon pulled from service.

In US Navy service the K-600 was labelled the HUK-1, with the prefix letter 'U' standing for utility. The primary job of the HUK-1 with the US Navy was to transport personnel and supplies between ships. It was powered by a piston engine that produced 600hp. Maximum speed was 101mph.

A New Medical Evacuation Helicopter

As a substitute for the Sikorsky S-51 helicopter that were being employed during the Korean War in the CASEVAC and CSAR roles, the US Army and the USMC took into service a Bell Aircraft Company commercial helicopter which the firm labelled the Bell 47.

The most numerous model of the Bell 47 series ordered was the three-person 'G' model assigned the designation OH-13H by the US Army and HTL-4 by the USMC. The letter prefix 'HTL' translates as helicopter/transport/Bell Aircraft Corporation/model number 4. All the variants of the Bell 47 in US Army service were later officially nicknamed the 'Sioux'. This was the first US Army helicopter series assigned an American Indian name, which is a tradition that continues to this day with one exception.

The most prominent design features of the Bell 47G were its Plexiglas goldfish bowl-like canopy, two large dorsal fuel tanks and its mostly exposed metal tail boom. It was powered by a piston engine that produced 245hp, which proved under-powered for operating in the mountains of Korea.

For the CASEVAC role the Bell 47G was fitted with two horizontal stretcher (litter) pods, one on either side of its lower fuselage. Approximately 700 units of the Sioux were eventually taken into the US Army inventory. A Bell 47G with the stretcher pods fitted was featured in the opening scene of the long-running American television series M*A*S*H.

From an article titled 'Helicopters in Combat: Korea' written by Dr Kenn Finlayson, in the 2001 summer issue of *Special Warfare Bulletin* published by the US Army, appears this passage on the worth of helicopters in the CASEVAC role:

> Rapid evacuation of seriously wounded soldiers directly from the front lines to the appropriate level of medical-evacuation chain significantly enhanced the survivability of soldiers. The fatality rate for seriously wounded soldiers, which had stood as 4.5 percent during World War II fell to 2.5 percent during the Korean War. Medevac pilots evacuated more than 20,000 casualties of all nationalities during the Korean War. 1st Lieutenant Joseph Bowler of the 2nd Helicopter Detachment evacuated 824 casualties between January 10 and November 2, 1951.

Post-Vietnam War Usage

The OH-13H/HTL-4 would be redesignated the UH-13H in 1962. It would remain in front-line service with the US Army and USMC until the late 1960s. During the early part of the Vietnam War, the US Army's UH-13H's primary role was as an observation platform. Vietnam War losses of the OH-13H totalled 174 units. It would end its post-Vietnam War days with the US Army in the training role.

The US Navy acquired twelve units of the Bell 47D and nine units of the Bell 47E variant. The former became the HTL-2 and the latter the HTL-3. The USAF acquired

---

1962 Helicopter Designation Changes

In 1962, the Department of Defense mandated that the US Army, US Navy and USMC adopt a new aircraft designation system based on that employed by the USAF. It was named the Tri-Service Aircraft Designation System and was back-dated to the earlier aircraft still in service in 1962.

Instead of an aircraft 'type' prefix letter being first in an aircraft's designation code, a basic mission prefix letter appears first and the aircraft type prefix letter second, which is always 'H' for helicopter. Examples include:

AH Attack Helicopter.
OH Observation Helicopter.
CH Transport (Cargo) Helicopter.
UH Utility Helicopter.
MH Multi-mission Helicopter (the prefix 'M' did not appear until 1977).
HH Search and Rescue or Hospital Helicopter.

The letter in alphabetical order following the aircraft design number stood for a minor design change that did not warrant a new design number. The letters 'I' and 'O' are not used in order to avoid confusion with the numbers '1' and '0'.

two examples of the commercial Bell 47 Ranger helicopter for VIP duties in 1957 and retired them in 1967.

Another Medical Evacuation Helicopter

Prior to the Korean War, the Hiller Aircraft Corporation had developed a small three-man helicopter which they labelled the UH-12. With the beginning of the Korean War the US Army began ordering the Hiller product as the H-23 and officially nicknamed it the 'Raven'.

The Raven was eventually fitted with a Plexiglas goldfish bowl-like canopy similar to that fitted to the Bell 47G and two horizontal stretcher pods, one on either side of its lower fuselage. It was powered by a piston engine that produced 250hp. Top speed was 95mph with a range of 205 miles. Service ceiling was 13,200ft.

The first three models of the Raven were designated by the US Army as H-23A, H-23B and H-23C, and were basically unmodified civilian versions. The following 'D' through to 'G' models were specially-built military versions, with the 'F' model having seating for four men.

By the time production of the Raven for the US Army concluded, it had acquired 1,681 units in a number of different versions. It would remain in US Army service long enough to see use during the early part of the Vietnam War in the observation role. A total of ninety-five units would be lost in Vietnam.

The US Navy also ordered a small number of the UH-12 labelled the HTE-1 and HTE-2, which translates as helicopter/transport/Hiller. With the advent of the Tri-Service Aircraft Designation System in 1962 the US Army H-13 Raven series became the OH-13 Raven series that translates as observation/helicopter.

Next in Line for Sikorsky

With a growing market for its helicopters in the immediate post-war years, Sikorsky developed a larger and more capable helicopter, which the company referred to as the S-55. It was powered by a piston engine that produced 389hp. The prototype had first flown in 1949. It had two pilots and could carry as many as eight passengers.

The USAF was very impressed and ordered 225 units, divided between models designated the H-19A and the H-19B, which entered into production in 1950. Many were tasked with the CASR/SAR role but none would remain in service long enough to see employment during the Vietnam War.

The US Army took into service a total of 373 units of the S-55 beginning in the early 1950s. Of that number, 72 units were designated the H-19C and the remaining 301 units were labelled the H-19D. Both were officially nicknamed the 'Chickasaw' by the US Army.

The USMC acquired 161 units of the S-55. The first 60 units that went to the USMC were labelled the HRS-1 and 101 units of a modified second version the

HRS-2. The translation for the designation code was 'H' for helicopter, 'R' for transport and the number representing the builder's sequential production number. Eventually the USMC took into service an improved HRS-3.

A description of the HRS-1 and its capabilities appears in this extract from a monograph titled *A History of Marine Medium Helicopter Squadron 161* written by Lieutenant Colonel Gary W. Parker:

> This 10-place aircraft was nearly 62 feet long counting the maximum extension of rotor blades, and 11.5 feet wide with the blades folded. The aircraft was designed to cruise at 90 knots [104mph] and had a gross weight of over 7,000 pounds at sea level ... Under field conditions in mountainous terrain, the HRS-1 could lift four to six troops with combat equipment, or it could lift up to 1,500 pounds of cargo or three to five casualties in litters.

The US Navy was also interested in the S-55 and would eventually order 119 units. The first ten units were labelled the HO4S-1 and entered service in 1950. Considered underpowered, the HO4S-1 was quickly replaced by seventy-nine units with a more powerful engine designated the HO4S-3. The US Navy would employ them primarily in the ASW role, operating from aircraft carriers.

Combat Usage in Korea

On 21 September 1951 the USMC employed its inventory of HRS-1 helicopters in Korea to transport 224 Marine infantrymen and 17,772lb of cargo to a mountain-top position overlooking the enemy forces in the area. It was referred to as Operation SUMMIT and was the first helicopter-borne landing of a combat unit in history.

From a USMC historical monograph titled *Whirlybirds: US Marine Helicopters in Korea* by Lieutenant Colonel Ronald J. Brown (retired) appears this extract on the shortcomings of the HRS series of helicopters:

> The HRS was a great step forward, but it was not the transport helicopter Marine planners envisioned. They wanted an aircraft that could carry fifteen or more men to ensure unit integrity during assaults and generating enough lift to carry most division equipment. The main problem with the HRS was lifting power. Although rated for eight passengers, in the harsh reality of the Korean mountains the HRS could only carry about six men – only four if they were fully combat-loaded.

For a couple of reasons the US Army was not able to deploy the H-19 Chickasaw series of helicopters to Korea until the final year of the conflict. Firstly, production delays meant there was a shortage of the new transport helicopter and secondly there was a serious jurisdictional controversy in 1951 between the USAF and the US Army on the use of the H-19 series helicopter as a troop transport. This issue was not resolved until after the Korean War when the US Army was allowed to employ helicopters in the troop transport role. This had been a mission the USAF had tried to reserve as its own.

Between May and June 1953, the senior US Army officer in Korea witnessed two large aerial supply exercises using the H-19 Chickasaw series. He was impressed enough to comment: 'The cargo helicopter, employed in mass, can extend the tactical mobility of the Army far beyond its normal capacity.' The same high-ranking army general went on to strongly recommend that the army make 'ample provisions for the full exploitation of the helicopter in the future.'

Another Helicopter Manufacturer Appears

In 1947, the US Navy took into service the first of twenty units of a Piasecki Aircraft Corporation utility helicopter the firm had labelled the PV-3. It was powered by a single engine that drove two overlapping rotors: one on the front of the fuselage and one at the rear.

The US Navy designated the PV-3 the HRP-1, which translates as helicopter/transport/Piasecki model 1. It had a crew of two and could carry up to ten passengers. Due to a host of unresolved design issues the US Navy eventually transferred most of its HRP-1 inventory to the USMC and the US Coast Guard. The helicopter's official nickname was the 'Harp'. An unofficial nickname was the 'sagging sausage'.

Those HRP-1s passed to the USMC formed the service's first helicopter-transport unit. The reason for the Corps' long-standing interest in troop transport helicopters appears in this passage from an article written by Douglas B. Nash Sr. titled 'Origins of the Gator Navy: Amphibious Shipping in Support of Landing Operations' published in a 2014 issue of *Fortitudine*, a bulletin of the Marine Corps Historical Program:

> With their greatly increased speed compared to amtracks [tracked amphibious troop transports] and latent troop-carrying potential, enough helicopters launched from dispersed platforms at sea could approach the landing area from different directions. By doing so, Marines could avoid enemy beach defenses altogether by going around their flanks and concentrating on the objective behind the beach defenses, thus achieving the mass needed to overcome the enemy without subjecting the initial assault waves to undue risk.

There were also four upgraded units of the HRP-1 which Piasecki designated the PV-17; these went directly to the US Coast Guard and were designated by them as the HRP-2. Both the HRP-1 and HRP-2 were powered by a 600hp piston engine.

A Progressively-Improved Model

Building on what it learned during the design and development of the HRP-2, Piasecki came up with an improved model. The US Navy designated it the HUP-1, which

One-Man Helicopter

Among the many different types of helicopters considered by the USMC at one time or another was the one-man helicopter that could be strapped to an infantry-man's back. The concept was translated into an operational requirement in 1952. Some of the general characteristics laid down for the proposed machine are:

1. Weight: 50–70lb.
2. Load-carrying Capacity: 240lb.
3. Operating Range: 10–15 miles.
4. Endurance: 15 minutes.
5. Speed: 30mph.
6. Minimum training by non-pilots.
7. Inexpensive.
8. Packaged in a one-man load and capable of being readied for flight by one man in not more than five minutes.
9. Capable of auto-rotation to a safe landing after an in-flight power failure.

A number of companies submitted their prototype one-man helicopters for USMC consideration. However, none could meet all the requirements set by the service. Either they were too heavy or impossible for non-pilots to master. In 1960, the commandant of the USMC decided that the concept of a one-man helicopter was impractical based on the existing technology and cancelled any further research on the project.

translates as helicopter/utility/Piasecki model one. The company-assigned name was 'Retriever'.

The 32 units of the HUP-1 that Piasecki built were followed by 394 units of an upgraded version labelled the HUP-2. Both were powered by piston engines that produced 550hp. The unofficial US Navy nickname for the HUP-1 and HUP-2 was the 'Hup-mobile' or 'Shoe' due to the shape of its fuselage.

One of the many jobs of the HUP-1 and HUP-2 was rescuing pilots and air crews that failed to successfully land on or take off from US Navy aircraft carriers. The job is referred to as being a 'plane guard'. During the Second World War that role was assigned to US Navy destroyers.

Eighteen units of the HUP-2 were later modified to see if they could be employed in the ASW role. That experiment was not a success as the helicopter proved under-powered for the job. The US Navy pulled the last of its inventory of Piasecki HUP series helicopters in 1964.

The US Army ordered seventy units of a modified HUP-2 helicopter in 1953, which was assigned the designation H-25A. It was given the official nickname 'Army Mule'.

The US Army was not impressed with the helicopter in service and fifty were therefore transferred to the US Navy in 1955. The navy relabelled them the HUP-3 and the rest went to foreign militaries.

Piasecki's Next-Generation Helicopter
On the heels of the Piasecki HUP-3 the USAF ordered the larger and longer Piasecki H-21, which the firm named the 'Workhorse'. It had first flown in 1952. The design layout of the H-21 mirrored that of the earlier Piasecki helicopters with a single piston engine powering two overlapping rotors at either end of the fuselage. Its unofficial military nickname was the 'Flying Banana' due to the shape of its fuselage, which is sometimes also applied to its two predecessors.

The thirty-two initial production units of the Piasecki Workhorse appeared in 1953 and were assigned the USAF designation H-21A. They were optimized for the CSAR/SAR role. The following 163 units of the H-21 ordered by the USAF had a more powerful engine that produced 1,425hp and were therefore labelled the H-21B. They were intended as transport helicopters, although some would later be modified for the CSAR role.

The USMC tested a total of six units of the H-21A in the troop transport role in 1952 but decided not to take any more into service or employ them during the Korean War. The US Army saw potential in the USAF H-21A as it could carry up to twenty fully-equipped soldiers in addition to its two pilots. It therefore ordered 334 units of the helicopter, designated the H-21C, and officially nicknamed it the 'Shawnee'.

With the Tri-Service Aircraft Designation System of 1962, the H-21C became the CH-21C, which translates as transport/helicopter. In USAF service the H-21B became the CH-21B in 1962.

Into Combat
The first US Army aviation units equipped with the Shawnee arrived in South Vietnam in 1961. At first the enemy was at a loss how to cope with the introduction of this new tactical troop transport helicopter. However, it did not take long for them

to understand its design limitations as seen in this extract from a report captured by the US Army at the time and translated:

> The disadvantages inherent in helicopters are difficult to overcome. If they are flown slow or low they are vulnerable to ground fire … the helicopter consumes much fuel, carrying a full load of troops its fuel capacity is reduced and as a consequence its range is reduced, as a result, the starting point for heliborne operations is usually near the objective and thus the enemy's element of surprise can be compromised.

As mentioned in the captured enemy report, the piston-engine-powered helicopters deployed to South Vietnam early on such as the Shawnee lacked the engine power to operate effectively in high temperatures or at higher altitudes, both of which prevailed in South Vietnam. This dropped their passenger complement from the original twenty to fewer than nine ARVN (Army of the Republic of Vietnam) soldiers.

Underpowered, large and slow, the Shawnee was extremely vulnerable to ever-improving enemy anti-aircraft defences. By 1964 this forced the US Army to pull them from front-line service in South Vietnam in favour of a smaller more modern helicopter with a gas turbine-powered engine. A total of thirty-six Shawnees were lost during the Vietnam War.

A New ASW Helicopter

The US Navy had had the foresight to place a back-up order in case the piston-engine Piasecki HUP-2 configured as an ASW helicopter did not live up to expectations. That back-up helicopter was the Sikorsky S-58, an enlarged and more formidable version of its earlier S-55 model. The piston engine on the S-58 produced 1,524hp.

The S-58 first entered US Navy service in 1955 as the HSS-1, which translates as helicopter/anti-submarine/Sikorsky model one. It was assigned the official nickname 'Seabat'. A total of 215 units of the Seabat were acquired by the US Navy, with an additional 167 units designated the HSS-1N specially designed for night and poor-weather flying conditions.

The Seabats worked in hunter-killer pairs, one equipped with the sonar equipment and the other armed with ASW weapons. The US Navy would later transfer some of its HSS-1N Seabats to the USAF, which employed them in the CSAR/SAR role. The US Navy also took into service 462 units of a utility version of the Seabat, which they referred to as HUS-1 and officially nicknamed the 'Seahorse'.

USMC Employment

The USMC acquired 603 new production units of the HUS-1, which were modified for their particular requirements. These entered into operational service with the USMC in 1957 and began showing up in South Vietnam in 1962. The HUS-1, which became the UH-34D in 1962, would be the primary troop transport of the USMC for most of the Vietnam War. An unofficial name for the UH-34D among Marines was 'Dog', based on the last letter of its designation.

An interesting note regarding the initial batch of UH-34Ds arriving in South Vietnam with the USMC is that the first thirty units were quickly transferred to the USAF. The USAF in turn provided them to the Central Intelligence Agency (CIA), which employed them under the auspices of 'Air America', a 'cover' airline operating in South-East Asia. The CIA used the former USMC UH-34D helicopters to perform a wide variety of covert operations.

The UH-34D was not the USMC's first choice for an assault troop transport but due to delays in acquiring the much larger and hopefully more capable assault troop transport the USMC desired, the UH-34D was adopted as an interim platform. The positive impression that the UH-34D made on the USMC is seen in this extract from an historical monograph titled *Marines and Helicopters 1962–1973* written by Lieutenant Colonel William R. Fails (retired):

> By its very reliability, simplicity, and capability, it seems to have given a new slang word to all Marines. When its more sophisticated cousins were grounded periodically for technical problems at the height of the war in Vietnam, the Marine on the ground could always give a radio call for assistance and specify a helicopter that he knew would respond. Using the old designation which never did lose its popularity among Marines and which was much easier to say over a radio, he would broadcast: 'Give me a HUS.'

In 1965, a small number of the USMC UH-34Ds in South Vietnam were fitted with an experimental add-on armament kit. The idea was they could act as ad hoc gun-ships and protect the standard troop transport variant of the UH-34D when USMC fixed-wing aircraft were not available. Field-testing of this arrangement was not a success and the idea was dropped, awaiting a more suitable helicopter. A total of 134 units of the UH-34D would be lost during the Vietnam War.

The USMC UH-34Ds were pulled from South Vietnam in 1969, with all the remaining units in the inventory being retired in 1972. In the 1987 movie *Full Metal Jacket*, directed and produced by Stanley Kubrick, four British Westland Wessex heli-copters (modified licence-built copies of the Sikorsky S-58, powered by a gas turbine engine) were acquired and repainted as USMC UH-34Ds employed during the Vietnam War.

US Army Employment

The US Army took into its inventory 380 units of a modified version of the basic S-58 beginning in 1955. They labelled it the H-34A and officially nicknamed it the 'Choctaw'. The H-34A became the CH-34A in 1962. It also came in a CH-34A and

S-58 Designation Changes

In 1962, with the advent of the Tri-Service Aircraft Designation System, all the variants of the S-58 that had entered into American military service were assigned new designations:

1. The US Navy HSS-1 Seabat became the SH-34G which translates as anti-submarine/helicopter.
2. The US Navy HSS-1N Seabat became the SH-34J, which translates as anti-submarine/helicopter.
3. The US Navy HSS-1N Seabats transferred to the USAF became the HH-34J, which translates as search and rescue/helicopter.
4. The US Navy HUS-1 Seahorse became the UH-34, which translates as utility/helicopter.
5. The USMC HUS-1 became the UH-34D, which translates as utility/helicopter.
6. The US Army H-34A Choctaw became the CH-34A, which translates as transport/helicopter.

CH-34D version. The US Army never deployed the Choctaw to South Vietnam and retired its inventory of Choctaws in the late 1960s.

S-56 Heavy-Lift Helicopter

Dwarfing all the American military helicopters that preceded it was the Sikorsky S-56. The prototype had first flown in 1953. It differed from earlier Sikorsky helicopters as it was powered by not one but two piston engines. The engines were located on either side of its fuselage in egg-shaped exterior pods with each engine producing 2,100hp.

The S-56 had been developed with the USMC in mind as an assault troop transport that could also bring in all the infantrymen's supporting weapons and equipment. It entered into operational service with the USMC in 1957 as the HR2S-1. Due to its twin-engine configuration it was unofficially nicknamed the 'Deuce' in USMC service.

When the Deuce was first envisioned, it was anticipated that the USMC would order 180 units. However, a continuing series of design and production delays meant that by the time it was deemed ready for operational service, the USMC dropped the order to only fifty-five units. During the interim period the USMC ordered more units of the HUS-1/UH-34D than originally planned to make up for the delay in fielding the Deuce. The latter was retired from USMC service in 1967.

The US Army was impressed with the S-56 and took ninety-four units into service, with the first entering service in 1958. The US Army assigned it the designation H-37A and officially nicknamed it the 'Mojave'. An upgrade of all but four of the H-37As in inventory resulted in the designation H-37B. In 1964, the US Army sent four of the

H-37B Mojave units to South Vietnam as flying tow-trucks. During their two years in theatre they recovered a total of 139 downed helicopters.

The Tri-Service Aircraft Designation System of 1962 resulted in the USMC HR2S-1 Deuce becoming the CH-37C. Those four US Army H-37As not upgraded to the 'B' standard became the CH-37A and the remaining ninety units of the H-37B received the designation CH-37B. The US Army retired their inventory of CH-37 series helicopters at approximately the same time that the USMC did theirs.

On display is this restored Sikorsky R-4B. It was the American military's first production helicopter, which entered into service in 1943. Just above the rear tail rotor of the R-4B is a model of its predecessor, the experimental VS-300. It first flew in tethered flight in September 1939 and in free flight in May 1940. (*Paul and Loren Hannah*)

(**Opposite, above**) The Sikorsky R-4Bs seen here had a service ceiling of 8,000ft and a top speed of 75mph. Their maximum range was 130 miles. The rear tail wheel prevented the tail rotor from striking the ground upon landing. Empty, the R-4B weighed 2,098lb. Its maximum take-off weight was 2,581lb. Those supplied to the British military were officially nicknamed the 'Hoverfly'. (*Department of Defense*, hereafter *DOD*)

(**Above**) For service at sea the Sikorsky R-4B was designated the HNS-1 and fitted with floats. The helicopter had a length of 48ft 1in and a height of 12ft 5in. The fuselage consists of metal tubing covered by fabric. The rotors were made of wood covered by fabric. The rotor diameter was 38ft 1in. (*US Coast Guard*)

(**Opposite, below**) The Sikorsky R-6A seen here was an upgraded R-4B with a streamlined metal fuselage and a more powerful engine. The combination of features provided the R-6A with a top speed of 100mph and a service ceiling of 10,000ft. It retained the side-by-side seating of the R-4B but came with a quadricycle landing gear. (*Paul and Loren Hannah*)

Pictured is a restored Sikorsky YH-5A with a tricycle landing gear. This was the USAAF designation for the first twenty-six production units of the helicopter with all the following production units being labelled the R-5A. The aircrew sat in tandem with the observer in front and the pilot behind him. The R-5A was redesignated the H-5A in 1949. *(USAF Museum)*

The restored USAF H-5D pictured was one of twenty redesigned units of the earlier R-5A. With it Sikorsky moved the pilot to the front of the fuselage and the observer behind him. It also came with an external rescue hoist and a quadricycle landing gear. The olive-drab paint scheme reflects its employment in the Korean War. *(Paul and Loren Hannah)*

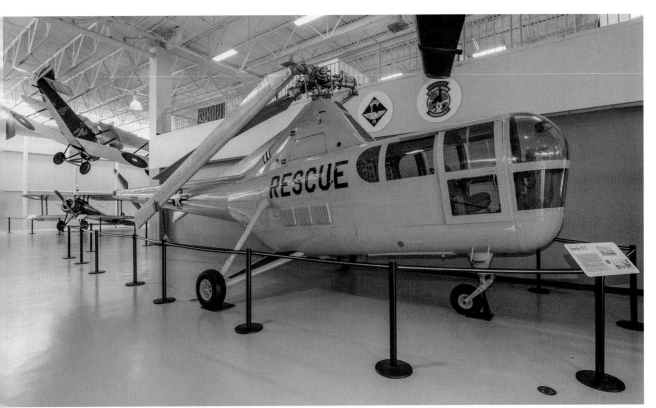

Sikorsky redesigned the H-5D to produce a larger and more capable version seen here that was labelled by the company as the S-51. An external spotting feature of the S-51 is the tricycle landing gear with a supporting strut for each of the two larger main wheel struts. The development of the helicopter was company-funded in the anticipation of both commercial and military orders. *(Paul and Loren Hannah)*

A landing signal officer (LSO) guides the pilot of the US Navy version of the Sikorsky S-51 labelled the HO3S-1 to a safe landing on the deck of an aircraft carrier. Due to a widened fuselage, the S-51 had a bench seat behind the pilot that could take three passengers. The first rescue of a US Navy pilot by the helicopter flying from a US Navy aircraft carrier CV-42, USS *Franklin D. Roosevelt* took place in February 1947. *(DOD)*

Early in the Korean War it was necessary for stretcher cases to be carried partially inside the S-51 fuselage. This is seen in this picture of a USMC model labelled the HO3S-1. The invention of the exterior fuselage stretcher pods proved to be a major improvement in the transporting of the wounded. On the opposite side of the helicopter can be seen the uppermost components of the rescue hoist. (DOD)

In this picture of an S-51 helicopter in USAF markings we see one of the factory-designed and built horizontal stretcher pods that appeared in service during the Korean War. In USAF service the S-51 was designated the H-5 series having three different versions. The crew of the helicopter is preparing the patient for a blood transfusion. (*DOD*)

The US Navy HO3S-1 pictured is on the USS *Philippine Sea* CV-47. The helicopter had a length of 57ft 1in and a height of 13ft with a rotor diameter of 48ft. The HO3S-1 had a top speed of 106mph and a range of 360 miles. Service ceiling for the aircraft was 14,000ft. Empty, the helicopter weighed 3,780lb with a maximum take-off weight of 4,825lb. (*DOD*)

(**Opposite, above**) The restored Sikorsky H05S seen here was the 1952 USMC replacement for the Sikorsky HO3S-1. There was room inside the helicopter's fuselage for two stretcher patients. They were loaded into the aircraft through the left-hand side of the Plexiglas front windshield, which was hinged and could be opened. In lieu of two stretcher patients, the aircraft could carry three passengers. (*Paul and Loren Hannah*)

(**Above**) Pictured on the flight deck of the US Navy aircraft carrier USS *Wright* CVL-49 are three units of the Bell HLT-2. It was the military counterpart of the Bell Model 47D helicopter and the first in that series to feature the goldfish bowl-like Plexiglas canopy. The US Navy acquired twelve units of the HLT-2 and nine units of a later model that Bell labelled the Model 47E and the US Navy the HLT-3. (*DOD*)

(**Opposite, below**) With continued production of the Bell 47 helicopter, a continuous series of external design changes was implemented for both the commercial and military versions. This can be seen here in a photograph of a US Army H-13 Sioux series helicopter. The original quadricycle landing gear has been replaced by two skids and the tail boom is no longer enclosed by fabric. (*DOD*)

(**Above**) The personnel of a US Army Mobile Army Surgical Hospital (MASH) during the Korean War pose with an H-13 Sioux series helicopter. It was the H-13 series that performed the majority of 17,700 aeromedical evacuations during the Korean War. As the helicopter had no cockpit lights, it was primarily employed during the hours of daylight. (*The National Archives*)

(**Opposite, above**) The US Army H-13 Sioux series helicopter pictured had a top speed of 105mph and a cruising speed of 84mph. It had a service ceiling of 10,500ft. The helicopter had a length of 31ft 7in, a height of 9ft 3in and its rotor diameter was 37ft 2in. Maximum range of the helicopter was 214 miles. (*DOD*)

(**Opposite, below**) The personnel of a US Army MASH unit are removing a patient from one of the two fuselage-attached stretcher pods on an H-13 Sioux series helicopter. As time went on, a heating system was devised for the stretcher pods. Patients with certain types of casts, splints and dressings could not be transported in these stretcher pods due to the confined space. (*DOD*)

Employment during the Korean War uncovered the fact that the engine on the US Army H-13 Sioux series helicopter seen here was unreliable and the electrical system was poorly-designed. This imposed a serious maintenance burden on those units equipped with the helicopter. Compounding the problems was the helicopter's limited range. (DOD)

For the use of the American president the USAF purchased two slightly-modified examples of the commercial Bell H-13J Ranger, one of which is seen here landing on the White House front lawn. The two modifications to the two presidential helicopters was the addition of all-metal rotor blades and a special anti-glare tinting for the Plexiglas at the front of the aircraft's fuselage. (USAF Museum)

The US Army had expressed no interest in the Hiller commercial Model 360 helicopter prior to the Korean War. This changed as the usefulness of the helicopter during the conflict pushed the US Army to order a large number of the Hiller Model 360 in several variants. In US Army service the helicopter was designated the H-23 Raven series. Pictured here is a restored example. *(Paul and Loren Hannah)*

On display is a Hughes TH-55 Osage. It was offered to the US Army in 1958 as a replacement for the aging OH-13 Sioux and the OH-23 Raven series helicopters. It was not judged suitable for a front-line observation helicopter. However, the US Army thought it would be the perfect training helicopter and eventually acquired 792 units that remained in service from 1964 to 1988. *(Paul and Loren Hannah)*

(**Above**) The innovative intermeshing and counter-rotating rotor system of the Kaman HOK-1 pictured in USMC markings did away with the need for an anti-torque tail rotor as used on all other helicopter designs. The three large vertical tail fins at the rear of the fuselage were for directional control. In US Navy service the helicopter was designated the HUK-1. (*DOD*)

(**Opposite, above**) The USAF was also impressed with the intermeshing and counter-rotating rotor system of the Kaman helicopter. It acquired their first units in 1958 and labelled it the H-43A Huskie. In 1962, the H-43A became the HH-43A. It differed from the versions flown by the USMC and US Navy as it had four large vertical tail fins at the rear of the fuselage, as seen in this photograph. (*DOD*)

(**Opposite, below**) As a replacement for its S-51 helicopter Sikorsky tried to come up with a larger version but failed in this endeavour. This pushed the firm's engineers to drop its evolutionary line of helicopter development and push forward with a more revolutionary helicopter design, which turned out to be the S-55 helicopter pictured here. In USAF service the helicopter was originally designated the H-19B. (*USAF Museum*)

(**Opposite, above**) Visible in this picture of a restored USAF H-19B series helicopter is the key difference between it and the Sikorsky helicopters that came before it. Rather than the engine being above and behind the flight crew, where access for maintenance was difficult, the engine was mounted in the lower front fuselage at an angle behind two clamshell doors for ease of access, with the pilots above and behind it. (*USAF Museum*)

(**Above**) Taking part in a simulated rescue is a USAF H-19B series helicopter that was redesignated the UH-19C in 1962. With the engine in the lower front of the fuselage it was possible to provide the S-55 with a spacious centre compartment with room for eight passengers. Sling-loaded, which is a method of suspending a load underneath the aircraft's fuselage, the S-55 could carry as much as 2,000lb of cargo. (*USAF Museum*)

(**Opposite, below**) In use with the US Navy as seen here the Sikorsky S-55 helicopter was labelled either the HO4S-1 with ten units built or the HO4S-3 with seventy-nine units built. The latter was fitted with a more powerful engine. In 1962, the HO4S-3 was redesignated the UH-19F. Maximum speed of the S-55 series was approximately 100mph with a range of 360 miles. (*DOD*)

(**Opposite, above**) On the flight deck of the US Navy aircraft carrier USS *Badoeng Strait* CVE-116 are a number of Sikorsky HO4S-3 helicopters. It is July 1954 and they are fitted for the anti-submarine role (ASW). In the air the helicopters worked in teams of two with one carrying the submarine detection gear and the other the weapons to destroy any undersea threats located. (*DOD*)

(**Opposite, below**) Pictured during the Korean War is a Sikorsky S-55 that was labelled the HRS-1 or HRS-2 by the USMC. It lacked the ASW detection gear and weapons of the US Navy version. In its place there were seats for eight passengers and self-sealing fuel tanks. In 1962, the last version of the series designated the HRS-3 was relabelled the CH-19E. (*DOD*)

(**Above**) On display at a US Army museum is this US Army version of the Sikorsky S-55 that was referred to as the H-19C Chickasaw. All four wheels on the helicopter were equipped with hydraulic shock absorbers. The pilots typically entered and left the cockpit from the outside of the aircraft via two step cut-outs on either side of the front fuselage. (*Paul and Loren Hannah*)

(**Opposite, above**) The US Navy became very interested in a tandem rotor prototype helicopter from Piasecki during the Second World War. This led to the 1947 fielding of the first of twenty-three units of a Piasecki helicopter designated the HRP-1 Harp by the US Navy and the 'Rescuer' by the builder. The example pictured here is one of three provided to the US Coast Guard by the US Navy and labelled the HRP-2. (*DOD*)

(**Opposite, below**) Wanting to test the capabilities of the new tandem-rotor Piasecki HRP-1 in the troop transport role, the USMC acquired five units. Unlike those employed by the US Navy and US Coast Guard which were constructed of steel tubing covered by fabric, those used in trials by the USMC were skinned with metal as seen in this picture. (*DOD*)

(**Above**) Entering into service with the US Navy beginning in 1949 was the Piasecki HUP Retriever helicopter series. Pictured here is an HUP-2 variant. It was the first helicopter acquired in large numbers by the US Navy, powered by a single engine that gave it a top speed of 105mph, a service ceiling of 10,000ft and a range of 340 miles. In 1962, it became the UH-25B. (*DOD*)

(**Above**) Pictured is a Piasecki HUP Retriever series helicopter often referred to by one of its unofficial nicknames as the 'Hup-mobile'. The name was borrowed from a car built up to 1940 by the Hupp Motor Car Company. The aircraft's primary role with the US Navy was shipboard utility purposes and as a 'plane guard' on US Navy carriers during launch or recovery of fixed-wing aircraft. (*Paul and Loren Hannah*)

(**Opposite, above**) The last model of the Piasecki HUP Retriever series helicopter was designated the HUP-3. A restored example is shown here. It had a length of 56ft 11in and a height of 12ft 7in. Empty it weighed 3,938lb and had a maximum take-off weight of 6,100lb. In 1962, the HUP-3 was relabelled the UH-25C. (*Paul and Loren Hannah*)

(**Opposite, below**) The US Army version of the Piasecki HUP-3 Retriever helicopter was designated the H-25A Army Mule. It had a flight crew of two and could carry up to five passengers. The US Army H-25A came with an enlarged circular door on the left-hand side of the fuselage as is visible in this picture of a restored example. (*Paul and Loren Hannah*)

(**Above**) A company photograph of an H-21B in USAF markings. The builder nicknamed it the 'Workhorse'. Reflecting its angled fuselage, it, like the earlier helicopters designed and built by Piasecki, was popularly nicknamed the 'Flying Banana'. The H-21A model was intended for both the general troop transport and the combat search and rescue (CSAR) role by the USAF. *(Piasecki)*

(**Opposite, above**) The US Army was impressed by the capabilities of the USAF Piasecki H-21B. They would therefore take into service after the Korean War a modified and upgraded version they labelled the H-21C Shawnee. It would be deployed to South Vietnam in late 1961. The following year, it became the CH-21C. *(DOD)*

(**Opposite, below**) Coming into a landing zone in South Vietnam are two US Army H-21C Shawnee helicopters. The helicopter's crew chief is visible in the aircraft's only door, no doubt holding a small-arm of some type. With a length of 66ft 4in and a height of 15ft 5in, it was a large hard-to-miss target for the enemy. *(DOD)*

The H-21C Shawnee helicopters that the US Army shipped to South Vietnam in late 1961 were not provided with any armament. However, it soon became clear that every helicopter needed the ability to provide itself with some sort of suppressive fire upon landing in a contested landing zone. Eventually the Shawnees began to be armed with small-calibre machine guns as seen here. (*DOD*)

ARVN soldiers are shown boarding a long line of US Army H-21C Shawnee helicopters. Like the Piasecki helicopters that came before it, the Shawnee was powered by a single engine. Its top speed was 131mph with a service ceiling of 7,750ft and a range of 400 miles. To ease the pilots' workload, it was fitted with an autopilot. (*DOD*)

A US Army H-21C Shawnee is shown with a sling-loaded 105mm howitzer minus its barrel. The Shawnee's single fuselage door visible in this photograph proved to be a problem during the Vietnam War. It restricted the speed with which the ARVN soldiers could disembark from the helicopter, making them and the helicopter highly vulnerable targets on the ground. (*DOD*)

(**Above**) On display at a US Army museum is this restored example of an H-21C Shawnee. During the Vietnam War the Shawnee helicopters were relatively safe as long as they flew above the effective range of enemy small-arms fire, which was approximately 2,000ft. On occasion large-calibre enemy anti-aircraft guns were encountered but this was rare during the early years of the conflict. (*Paul and Loren Hannah*)

(**Opposite, above**) The orange bars on the US Army H-21C Shawnee helicopter in the foreground and visible on the parked helicopters in the background identified them as training aircraft. During the Vietnam War it was not unheard of for the enemy to both mine and drive large wooden stakes into the ground at potential landing sites for US military helicopters. (*DOD*)

(**Opposite, below**) The US Navy replacement for the Sikorsky S-55 in the ASW and transport roles was an enlarged and more powerful version that the firm labelled the S-58. The US Navy took the first production units into service in 1954. It came in two different versions. One model intended for the utility role was designated the HSS-1 Seahorse with an example shown here. (*DOD*)

(**Above**) The ASW version of the S-58 was referred to by the US Navy as the HSS-1 Seabat. An example is pictured here with its dipping sonar deployed. To assist the pilots in maintaining a steady hover while the sonar operator listened for submarines, the helicopter had a flight stabilization system. The sonar unit was lowered and raised by a hydraulically-operated reel and cable system. (*DOD*)

(**Opposite, above**) When the US Navy versions of the Sikorsky S-58 entered service in the early 1950s, the USMC took notice. The Corps did not see the S-58 as an assault troop transport, since it was then interested in much larger helicopters for that role. Rather, they saw the S-58 as a useful utility helicopter for moving supplies from ship to shore. A version taken into service as the HUS-1 is pictured here. (*DOD*)

(**Opposite, below**) In the foreground a USMC HUS-1 Seahorse is shown pulling astronaut Virgil Grissom from the ocean following splashdown after the MR-4 suborbital flight of July 1961. In the background is a US Navy HSS-1 Seabat, as indicated by the various ASW detection gear components under its fuselage. The first units of the HUS-1 entered operational service with the USMC in 1957. By this time it was no longer seen as a simple utility helicopter but as an assault troop transport. (*DOD*)

(**Above**) Marines are shown here awaiting their turn to board a landing HUS-1. The helicopter was switched from the utility to the assault troop transport role by the USMC due to delays in the fielding of a much larger Sikorsky assault troop transport helicopter. The original USMC plans called for the HUS-1 to serve only as a stop-gap assault troop transport until the larger helicopter entered service. (*DOD*)

(**Opposite, above**) Marine infantrymen are seen here being directed to board on a waiting line of HUS-1 helicopters by US Navy personnel. Post-Korean War, the US Navy began modifying some of its older-generation aircraft carriers into specialized amphibious assault ships. In this new role they were referred to as a Landing Platform Helicopter (LPH). (*DOD*)

(**Opposite, below**) A formation of USMC HUS-1 helicopters heads out on a training mission, having taken off from USS *Boxer* LPH-4 seen in the background. The HUS-1's rotor was 56ft in diameter and worked together with a smaller 9ft 6in anti-torque rotor on the fuselage tail. For ease of storage aboard ship the four rotor blades could be manually folded back to conserve space. (*DOD*)

As with almost all American military helicopters that saw service during the Vietnam War, the USMC UH-34D was eventually armed with small-calibre machine guns, as seen in this photograph. Originally, the only armament on the helicopter might have been two submachine guns; one for the co-pilot and one for the crew chief. (*DOD*)

(**Opposite, above**) A trio of USMC HUS-1 helicopters is preparing to land to pick up passengers sometime during the Vietnam War. In 1962, the HUS-1 became the UH-34D. The passenger compartment on the helicopter was 13ft long, 5ft wide and 6ft high with a large sliding door on the right side of the fuselage. There was seating for a maximum of twelve passengers. (*DOD*)

(**Opposite, below**) Disembarking from a USMC HUS-1 helicopter on board a US Navy aircraft carrier is American President Dwight D. Eisenhower. Both the USMC and US Army employed specially-modified versions of the S-58 helicopter for presidential use beginning in 1959 and continuing into the early 1960s. Note the emergency amphibious pontoons on the front wheels of the helicopter. (*DOD*)

(**Opposite, above**) In US Army service the S-58 helicopter was designated the H-34A Choctaw. It was 56ft long and had a height of 15ft 11in. The top speed was 123mph with a range of 250 miles and a service ceiling of 9,515ft. Empty it weighed 7,900lb with a take-off weight of 14,000lb. However, as with all helicopters, there could be variations in these figures. (DOD)

(**Opposite, below**) Marked with the orange bands of a training helicopter is a US Army H-34A Choctaw. It was the first Sikorsky helicopter to be subjected to wind tunnel testing to optimize its aerodynamic shape in a bid to reduce drag and increase speed. The four-blade main rotor system was chosen to increase speed and reduce vibration. (DOD)

(**Above**) Seen here is a CH-37B Mojave, which first entered US Army service in 1956. It was a massive aircraft designed and built by Sikorsky, with a length of 64ft 3in and a height of 22ft. Two engines powered a single rotor that had a diameter of 72ft. The helicopter's top speed was 130mph with a range of 145 miles and a service ceiling of 8,700ft. (DOD)

(**Opposite, above**) The Sikorsky US Army CH-37B Mojave had a spacious cargo compartment capable of carrying up to twenty-six passengers or small wheeled vehicles as demonstrated in this picture. It was this passenger-carrying capacity that had sparked the USMC to order it into production in 1951 as the HR2S. Due to design issues it did not enter operational service with the USMC until 1956 as the HR2S-1. (*Paul and Loren Hannah*)

(**Opposite, below**) Too large and slow to operate as a troop transport in South Vietnam, the Sikorsky US Army CH-37B Mojave served in the aircraft recovery role as seen here during the Vietnam War until replaced by more efficient gas turbine helicopters. Empty, the helicopter weighed 20,831lb and had a maximum take-off weight of 31,063lb. Within its interior cargo compartment 2,000lb of goods could be carried. (*DOD*)

(**Above**) In this picture a USMC HR2S-1 is being refuelled. In 1962, it became the CH-37C. By the time it reached service with the USMC the reign of the piston engine-powered helicopter was nearing its end and only a minimum number was ordered by the Corps as they knew the future lay in gas turbine engine-powered helicopters. (*DOD*)

Chapter Two

Gas Turbine Engine Transport Helicopters

The usefulness of the utility helicopters employed by the American military during the Korean War was offset by the poor reliability of their reciprocating engines and their low power-to-weight ratio. The US Army therefore set a requirement in 1954 for a next-generation utility helicopter with a more reliable and powerful gas turbine engine. The first production gas turbine engine-powered helicopter was French and flew in 1956.

The advantages of gas turbine engines were numerous. They had far fewer parts than their piston-engine counterparts, which made them more reliable. They were also dramatically smaller and lighter, and produced a much higher power-to-weight ratio than reciprocating engines. Unlike piston engines that required costly high-octane gasoline, gas turbine engines can run on a wide variety of less costly and more readily available fuels.

The Huey Arrives on Scene

A number of companies responded to the US Army's 1954 requirement for a new gas turbine-powered helicopter for the aerial ambulance (MEDEVAC) role. Medical care is provided on helicopters employed for the MEDEVAC mission by a military attendant with a degree of medical training.

It was originally intended that the proposed new gas turbine helicopter would also be the replacement for the H-13 Raven and the H-19 Chickasaw in the observation role. Secondary duties envisioned for this new helicopter would include training and liaison work. At the time there was no thought of employing it as a troop transport.

In 1955 the US Army selected a Bell Helicopter submission that the manufacturer labelled the Model 204. After extensive testing and numerous design changes it was adopted in 1959 as the HU-1A, which translates to helicopter/utility/model 1. Impressed by its performance during trials, the US Army soon saw it as the replacement for the H-34 Choctaw and the H-21 Shawnee in the troop transport role. ⤸

The HU-1A was officially assigned the nickname 'Iroquois'. Its unofficial nickname, much more popular throughout its service career and right up to the present day, is the 'Huey'. The HU-1A had a crew of two and could carry six seated passengers in the troop transport role. Its engine provided 770hp. A total of 182 were ordered for the US Army.

Next in Line

Even as the HU-1A model entered the inventory the US Army had Bell begin work on the HU-1B. It was fitted with a more powerful engine that produced 960hp and an enlarged passenger compartment. It had a crew of four – two pilots and two crew chiefs/door gunners – and could carry eight seated passengers. It began entering service in 1961 with a total of 1,014 units constructed for the US Army. With the 1962 Tri-Service Aircraft Designation System the HU-1A became the UH-1A and the HU-1B the UH-1B.

The USMC ordered a modified version of the UH-1B in 1962 which they designated the UH-1E. It was the replacement for the Korean War-vintage OH-43D, and was a small fixed-wing observation aircraft. The first of 194 production units began coming off the assembly line in 1964. Later-production units of the USMC UH-1Es were based on a 'C' model Huey. However, the USMC retained the UH-1E designation for both models. Of the USMC UH-1Es that served during the Vietnam War, 100 units were lost.

An important difference between the US Army UH-1B and the USMC UH-1E is described in this passage from an historical monograph titled *Marines and Helicopters 1962–1973* written by Lieutenant Colonel William R. Fails (retired):

> The UH-1E was constructed of aluminum. Most helicopter designers previously had relied on magnesium to fabricate parts of a helicopter, since the lightness of the metal improved the payload capability of the aircraft and more than compensated for magnesium's inflammability (illumination flares usually are made of magnesium due to the ease of ignition, rapid burning with bright light, and the ability of the metal to burn even under water) and tendency to corrode when exposed to salt air or water. If this corrosion was not halted, the metal soon disintegrated into a pile of white dust.

Into Combat

In 1962, the UH-1B model began showing up in South Vietnam configured either for the MEDEVAC or troop transport roles. Some were also modified to serve as gunships. This passage from a US Army publication titled *Vietnam Studies: Airmobility 1961–1971* by Lieutenant General John J. Tolson (retired) describes what the UH-1B brought to the Vietnam War as a troop transport:

> When the UH-1B transport helicopter was first introduced in Vietnam, it usually carried ten combat-equipped Vietnamese soldiers and at times as many as eleven. An investigation determined that the average helicopter was grossly

overloaded with as many soldiers … Not only that, the center of gravity has shifted beyond safe limits. As a consequence, the standard procedure was to limit the UH-1B to eight [ARVN] combat troops except in grave emergencies.

Despite the more efficient and powerful gas turbine engines, the temperature and elevation extremes of South Vietnam sometimes badly degraded the operational performance of both the UH-1A and the UH-1B. This led to many complaints from those in the field who depended on these early Huey models for a variety of tasks.

Model 'D' Huey

The performance shortfalls of the UH-1A and UH-1B pushed the manufacturer to redesign the helicopter. This resulted in the 41in longer UH-1D, powered by a 1,100hp engine that could carry more passengers or stretcher cases. The UH-1D first arrived in South Vietnam in 1964 and was primarily employed as a troop transport that replaced the CH-21C Shawnees. It had a crew of four – two pilots and two crew chiefs/door gunners – and could carry eleven seated passengers.

To facilitate the entry and departure of passengers from the UH-1D, the helicopter was fitted on either side of its fuselage with larger sliding doors, which were sometimes completely removed in the field. The two pilots of the UH-1D had armoured seats, but not the passengers.

Unfortunately the UH-1D still lacked the lifting power to operate effectively in many areas of South Vietnam. A total of 2,561 units of the 'D' model Huey were built for the US Army. Of that number, 1,926 went on to see service during the Vietnam War with 886 lost during the conflict.

Model 'H' Huey

It took the 1967 introduction of a UH-1H model powered by a 1,400hp engine before the US Army felt that the helicopter's design had reached the performance benchmarks required by the service. The UH-1H was basically a modified UH-1D. Besides having a more powerful engine, the UH-1H was also instrumented to allow its pilots to fly at night or in poor weather conditions.

A total of 5,435 units of the UH-1H were eventually acquired by the US Army, many of which were rebuilt UH-1Ds. Of all the various UH-1 models that would serve during the Vietnam War, the UH-1H was the most numerous with 3,375 spending time in theatre and 1,313 of those being lost. In Vietnam the UH-1H could carry as many as twelve seated ARVN soldiers or up to nine seated US Army soldiers. The last UH-1H was pulled from US Army service in 2012.

The USAF acquired thirty examples of the UH-1H designated the HH-1H for the CSAR role. There were also twenty-two units of the UH-1H employed by the USAF that were configured for both interception and jamming of enemy radio communication. These were designated the EH-1H, with the prefix letter 'E' standing for

Leave No Man Behind

The Huey helicopter performed yeoman duty during the Vietnam War and became the symbol to many of the conflict. However, not to be forgotten are the brave men who operated those aircraft in the face of extreme danger to themselves. One of those was US Army Lieutenant Colonel Charles S. Kettles (retired) who was awarded the Medal of Honor in July 2016 by the president of the United States. His citation below reflects the 'no man left behind' ethos of the American armed forces:

'On 15 May 1967, [then] Major Kettles, upon learning that an airborne infantry unit had suffered casualties during an intense firefight with the enemy, immediately volunteered to lead a flight of six UH-1D helicopters to carry reinforcements to the embattled force and to evacuate wounded personnel. Enemy small arms, automatic weapons, and mortar fire raked the landing zone, inflicting heavy damage to the helicopters; however, Major Kettles refused to depart until all helicopters were loaded to capacity. He then returned to the battlefield, with full knowledge of the intense enemy fire awaiting his arrival, to bring more reinforcements, landing in the midst of enemy mortar and automatic weapons fire that seriously wounded his gunner and severely damaged his aircraft.

Upon departing, Major Kettles was advised by another helicopter crew that he had fuel streaming out of his aircraft. Despite the risk posed by the leaking fuel, he nursed the damaged aircraft back to base. Later that day, the Infantry Battalion Commander requested immediate emergency extraction of the remaining forty troops, including four members of Major Kettles' unit who were stranded when their helicopter was destroyed by enemy fire. With only one flyable UH-1 helicopter remaining, Major Kettles volunteered to return to the deadly landing zone for a third time, leading a flight of six evacuation helicopters, five of which were from the 161st Aviation Company.

During the extraction, Major Kettles was informed by the last helicopter that all personnel were onboard, and departed the landing zone accordingly. Army gunships supporting the evacuation also departed the area. Once airborne, Major Kettles was advised that eight troops had been unable to reach the evacuation helicopters due to the intense enemy fire. With complete disregard for his own safety, Major Kettles passed the lead to another helicopter and returned to the landing zone to rescue the remaining troops. Without gunship, artillery, or tactical aircraft support, the enemy concentrated all firepower on his lone aircraft, which was immediately damaged by a mortar round that shattered both front windshields and the chin bubble and was further raked by small arms and machine gun fire. Despite the intense enemy fire, Major Kettles maintained control of the aircraft and situation, allowing time for the remaining eight soldiers to board the aircraft. In spite of the severe damage to his helicopter, Major Kettles once more skillfully guided his heavily damaged aircraft to safety.

Without his courageous actions and superior flying skills, the last group of soldiers and his crew would never have made it off the battlefield. Major Kettles' selfless acts of repeated valor and determination are in keeping with the highest traditions of military service and reflect great credit upon himself and the United States Army.'

electronics. Twenty-seven units of a US Navy version of the UH-1H were configured for the CSAR role and labelled the HH-1K.

Other Huey Models in the Vietnam War

Seeing service during the Vietnam War in very small numbers were other specialized Huey models. These included the UH-1F, a USAF model of the UH-1B of which 119 were ordered with the first entering service in 1964. Some were eventually converted to gunships and labelled the UH-1P. The UH-1F was powered by a 1,100hp engine and combined design features of both the UH-1B and UH-1D.

The UH-1L was a US Navy version of the USMC UH-1E, of which eight were built with two seeing service during the Vietnam War. The UH-1M was a UH-1C gunship with a more powerful engine fitted, five of which made it to South Vietnam. The first Huey with a dual-engine arrangement was the UH-1N, of which only two made it to South Vietnam before American armed forces withdrew in 1973. It was essentially an upgraded UH-1H.

Post-Vietnam War Huey Helicopters

Deliveries of 294 units of the UH-1Ns began in 1970 to the USAF and USMC, with the latter taking the majority. There were six units of a VIP transport version of the UH-1N designated the VH-1N for the USMC. In service the UH-1N acquired the unofficial nickname of the 'Twin Huey'.

A modified version of the UH-1N for USAF counterinsurgency operations (COIN) was designated the HH-1N. The two coupled engines on the helicopter produced 1,800hp. In 2005, the USAF took into its inventory the first of twenty-four rebuilt and upgraded UH-1H helicopters for the training role for which they were redesignated the TH-1H.

In 2016, the USAF still retained fifty-nine units of the UH-1N in its inventory. A description of the many roles performed by the UH-1N appears in this extract from an official USAF online fact sheet:

> The UH-1N is a light-lift utility helicopter used to support various missions. The primary missions include: airlift of security forces, security and surveillance of off-base nuclear weapon convoys, and distinguished visitor airlift. Other uses include: disaster response operations, medical evacuation, airborne cable inspection, support to aircrew survival school, aerial testing, routine missile site support and transport.

The USMC phased out the last of its UH-1Ns in 2014. Its replacement, deliveries of which began in 2009, is a redesigned and upgraded model labelled the UH-1Y and officially nicknamed the 'Venom'. It was originally planned to base the 107 units of the Venom on rebuilt UH-1Ns but only 10 were completed before it was decided to have the remaining helicopters built from new. The Venom is often configured as a command and control (C&C) platform but also has a secondary mission as a gunship.

The US Army Searches for Something New

In 1956, the US Army announced to industry that it was looking for a gas turbine engine-powered medium-lift transport helicopter. Boeing Vertol submitted a helicopter prototype they referred to as the V-107, which could carry twenty passengers. Three examples of the two-engine, tandem-rotor helicopter were assigned the designation YHC-1A by the US Army during testing, which began in 1958.

The US Army eventually rejected the Boeing Vertol YHC-1A for a couple of reasons. Firstly it was felt that it was too large and heavy for the infantry assault role, and secondly too small and light to transport the service's towed artillery pieces and the new Pershing surface-to-surface missile system. Instead, the US Army decided on the lengthened Bell UH-1D for the infantry assault role and once again began looking for a suitable medium-lift transport helicopter.

USMC Interest

Nevertheless, all was not lost for Boeing Vertol. The USMC had identified a requirement in 1960 for a HUS-1/UH-34D troop transport replacement and liked the YHC-1A. To meet the USMC requirements, it had to be redesigned to such an extent that it was basically a new helicopter, designated the HRB-1. In 1962, the HRB-1 became the CH-46A and was assigned the official nickname 'Sea Knight'.

The advantages of the CH-46A over its predecessor appear in this passage from a monograph titled *A History of Marine Medium Helicopter Squadron 161* written by Lieutenant Colonel Gary W. Parker:

> The CH-46 could lift more than double the payload of the UH-34D. A tandem-rotor helicopter, it could carry a crew of three and 17–25 fully equipped troops

or 4,000 pounds of cargo over a combat radius of 115 miles at 150 miles per hour. The CH-46 could also be configured to carry up to 15 litter patients. The fuselage was sealed to allow water operations, and it had a large rear ramp for straight-in loading of vehicles and bulky freight.

The CH-46A Sea Knight began entering operational service with the USMC in 1963, 160 units having been ordered by the Corps. It was powered by two engines, each producing 1,250hp. However, there were design flaws with the 'A' model of the Sea Knight and these caused a number of serious accidents that resulted in a number of add-on modifications to the helicopter.

Improved Sea Knights

The USMC eventually ordered 266 units of an improved version designated the CH-46D. It arrived in South Vietnam in 1967 and was powered by two engines, each producing 1,400hp. In a monograph titled *Marines and Helicopters 1962–1973* written by Lieutenant Colonel William R. Fails (retired) appears this passage on what the CH-46D Sea Knight had brought to the USMC during its time in service:

> With the arrival in Vietnam of the first 'D's, and with the correction of its structural problems, the CH-46 at last was ready to take its place as the heart of the Marines' vertical lift capability, not only in Vietnam but throughout the world. Uncounted Marines since 1967 have conducted assaults from them, depended for food, water, and ammunition upon them, and have returned to their home bases in them. Countless Marines owe their lives to the CH-46, which picked up the wounded – often in the face of enemy fire – and sped them to waiting hospitals.

Reflecting its many decades in service, the USMC never stopped having the builder improve and upgrade its inventory of CH-46 Sea Knight series helicopters. This would result in the CH-46F entering service with the Corps between 1968 and 1971. It in turn would be superseded by the CH-46E, the last model of the series in USMC service. It consisted of 147 new-built examples and the rebuilding of 275 older models. The CH-46E was retired from USMC service in 2014.

US Navy Employment of the Sea Knight

The US Navy originally took into its inventory fourteen units of the CH-46A, which it designated the UH-46A and employed in the utility role, transporting cargo and personnel between ships. Approximately 50 of the original 160 units of the USMC CH-46A inventory were later acquired by the US Navy for the CSAR role and labelled the HH-46A.

In 1966, the US Navy took into service a utility version of the CH-46D that they labelled the UH-46D. The service eventually took all the remaining UH-46As, and some of its UH-46Ds, and configured them for the CSAR role with such additions as an external rescue hoist. The US Navy pulled all its remaining Sea Knight series helicopters from service in 2004.

Osprey

The USMC replacement for the Sea Knight series was the tiltrotor MV-22B, officially nicknamed the 'Osprey'. The design and building of the aircraft is shared by Bell and Boeing. The Osprey is both faster and has greater range than its predecessor. It takes off vertically, or in a short take-off and landing mode. Once airborne, the nacelle (engine and prop-rotor group) on each wing rotates into a forward position, which effectively converts it from a helicopter into a fixed-wing aircraft.

The first flight of the MV-22B Osprey was in 1989, with approval for its production granted in 2005. The aircraft reached operational service with the USMC in 2007. The US Navy has committed to buying forty-four units of a modified version of the MV-22B Osprey employed by the USMC. The first production units are to be delivered in 2022 with the designation CMV-22B.

Chinook

Because the US Army was not interested in the Boeing Vertol YHC-1A design, the company offered the service a larger and more advanced helicopter prototype they labelled the Model 114. For testing purposes the US Army designated the twin-engine, tandem-rotor prototype as the YHC-1B.

Trials of the YHC-1B began in 1961 and went sufficiently well for the US Army to order it into production as the HC-1B. In 1962, it became the CH-47A and was officially nicknamed the 'Chinook'. The first of 349 CH-47As entered US Army service in 1962. The initial engines fitted to the 'A' model produced 2,200hp each. They were soon replaced by engines that produced 2,650hp each.

The 'A' model was followed off the assembly line by 108 units of a progressively-improved model designated the CH-47B. The 'B' model had engines that each produced 2,850hp. Both models of the Chinook saw service during the Vietnam War. They had a crew of three: two pilots and a loadmaster. Chinooks could carry as many as thirty-one seated passengers or up to fifty-five standing passengers.

A description of one of the many roles of the two early models of the Chinook during the Vietnam War appears in this extract from a US Army publication titled *Vietnam Studies: Airmobility 1961–1971* by Lieutenant General John J. Tolson (retired):

> The most spectacular mission in Vietnam for the Chinook was the placing of artillery batteries in perilous mountain positions that were inaccessible by any other means, and then keeping them resupplied with large quantities of ammunition … The Chinook soon proved to be such an invaluable aircraft for artillery

movement and heavy logistics that it was seldom used as an assault troop carrier.

Upon its arrival in South Vietnam in 1965, the Chinook also eventually took over the role of recovering downed aircraft that had previously been performed by the CH-37 Mojave series. It was also occasionally employed for recovering US Army wheeled and light tracked vehicles that could not be recovered by normal methods.

Post-Vietnam War Chinooks

The Chinook has gone through a series of progressively-improved models during its time in service with the US Army. In 1974, there appeared the first units of the CH-47C, of which 233 were ordered. It was followed off the production line by 472 units of the CH-47D.

The 'D' model of the Chinook was not new-built as were the previous versions. Rather, all the CH-47D were rebuilds of the first three models of the helicopter, except for two units. The first CH-47D appeared in US Army service in 1979.

The CH-47D has in turn been superseded by approximately 200 units of a modernized version that is designated the CH-47F, which first came off the assembly line in 2001. The US Army hopes to obtain funding to acquire a total of 464 units of the 'F' model Chinook.

To ease the pilot's workload and improve the helicopter's handling in the air, the 'F' model of the Chinook has a Digital Automatic Flight Control System (DAFCS). In addition, the CH-47F comes with a new monolithic airframe structure to reduce cockpit vibration and increase airframe durability.

Sea Stallion

Like the US Army, the USMC desired a gas turbine engine-powered replacement for their version of the piston engine-powered CH-37. This resulted in the delivery, beginning in 1966, of the first of 139 units of a Sikorsky-designed twin-engine helicopter that the firm designated the S-65. Each engine produced 2,850hp. The USMC labelled it the CH-53A and officially nicknamed it the 'Sea Stallion'.

The CH-53A Sea Stallion first arrived in South Vietnam in 1967. It was capable of carrying as many as thirty-eight seated Marine infantrymen or up to ninety standing ARVN soldiers. As recounted by Judd Hilton, former Sea Stallion pilot, in the book titled *Vietnam: The Helicopter War* by Philip D. Chinnery, there was always an element of danger in transporting ARVN soldiers:

> After we would unload the ARVNs we would have to go through the entire helicopter before we took off, to ensure they had not planted a grenade in the helicopter. On three occasions we found them and it happened routinely to everybody ... they were definitely trying to kill us.

In spite of its impressive passenger-carrying abilities, the Sea Stallion was primarily intended as a flying tow truck. In 1967, it recovered 370 aircraft. Befitting the helicopter's impressive lifting abilities, some applied the unofficial nickname to it of the 'Super Bird'.

Also seeing service in the Vietnam War was the improved CH-53D, of which the USMC ordered 126 units. Each of its engines produced 3,925hp. It had been redesigned to provide seating for as many as fifty-five passengers if the need arose. The USMC would lose nineteen units of the CH-53 series Sea Stallion during the Vietnam War. The last of the Sea Stallions was retired from USMC service in 2012.

Super Stallion

In the belief that bigger was better, the USMC went on to acquire a larger three-engine version of the two-engine Sea Stallion. This new three-engine Sikorsky-designed-and-built helicopter was labelled by the manufacturer as the S-80 and by the USMC as the CH-53E. It was assigned the official nickname 'Super Stallion' and first appeared in operational service with the USMC in 1981. It was also acquired in small numbers by the US Navy as a heavy-lift transport.

In total the USMC took into service 170 units of the Super Stallion with plans to keep the remaining units in the inventory until 2027. What the Super Stallion brings to the USMC is described in this passage from an official online site for the Corps:

> The heavy-lift helicopter of the Marine Corps can carry a 26,000-pound Light Armored Vehicle, 16 tons of cargo 50 miles and back, or enough combat-loaded Marines to lead an assault or humanitarian operation; but perhaps what's most amazing about the largest military helicopter in the U.S. is what it achieves despite its size. Though powerful enough to lift every aircraft in the Marine inventory except the KC-130 [four-engine transport plane], the CH-53E Super Stallion is compact enough to deploy on amphibious assault ships, and has the armament, speed, and agility to qualify as much more than a heavy lifter.

A Much-Needed Alternative

The replacement of the CH-53E Super Stallion has been of prime importance to the USMC as age and heavy operational use have taken their toll on the inventory. This has forced the USMC to take some of its CH-53E helicopters out of retirement for operational use and others to be stripped for their parts. Sikorsky's answer has been the development of a new state-of-the-art model of the CH-53 family of helicopters, which the Marines have designated the CH-53K and assigned the official nickname 'King Stallion'.

The first flight of the newly-built King Stallion took place in 2015 with production set to begin in 2018. The USMC plans to acquire an inventory of approximately 200 units of the helicopter between 2018 and 2022. The addition of a more powerful engine will allow it to carry a maximum of 30,000lb of cargo internally and 88,000lb externally. The CH-53E is limited to 8,265lb internally and 27,000lb externally. The CH-53K at 195.6mph is a bit faster than the 172.5mph of the CH-53E.

Huey Replacement

Despite its useful service during the Vietnam War, the US Army felt that Huey helicopter losses were unacceptably high. Of the 7,013 Huey helicopters that served during the Vietnam War, a total of 3,305 were lost. This in turn caused the death of 1,074 pilots and 1,103 flight crew members. In addition, 532 American military passengers perished on board Huey helicopters. This pushed the US Army during the conflict to start thinking about a more survivable troop transport helicopter to replace the Huey.

In 1972, the US Army issued a requirement for a Huey replacement under the Utility Tactical Transport Aircraft System (UTTAS) programme and a number of manufacturers submitted proposals. Of those, the US Army chose Sikorsky and Boeing Vertol to submit prototypes for testing. Upon the conclusion of those tests it was announced in 1976 that the Sikorsky product, which the firm labelled the S-60, was the superior helicopter.

Into Service

The first production example of the S-60 flew in 1978. In US Army service it was designated the UH-60A and officially named the 'Black Hawk'. Each of the two engines on the UH-60A produced some 1,560hp. It had a crew of four (two pilots and two crew chiefs/door gunners) and was authorized to carry up to eleven seated passengers. In an emergency it could carry as many as twenty non-seated passengers.

Between 1977 and 1989, the US Army took into its inventory a total of 974 units of the UH-60A. It was replaced on the production line in 1989 by the UH-60L, with each engine producing 1,890hp. The UH-60L, or 'Lima', based on its radio-alphabet code word, was built until 2007, with approximately 500 units entering the US Army inventory.

In 2001, the US Army decided that its UH-60L fleet would be replaced by a new state-of-the-art model of the Black Hawk designated the UH-60M. It was originally planned to base all the new UH-60M helicopters on the rebuilding of 1,500 units of the 'A' and 'L' model Black Hawks. Eventually it was decided by the US Army that 1,227 new-built units of the UH-60Ms were more cost-effective than rebuilding the earlier model inventory. The new-built 'M' model Black Hawk helicopter first entered service in 2006. The engines on this newest version of the Black Hawk series each produce 2,000hp.

A description of what the UH-60M brought to the US Army helicopter crews in Afghanistan appears in a quote by Lieutenant Colonel Jerry Davis, product manager for UH-60 Modernization, which appeared in a US Army online article dated 4 March 2010:

> We went from analogue type displays on the dash to multifunction digital displays. Now, the aircraft has a moving map capability with digital situational awareness … It gave pilots a better awareness of where their units were, where their supportive units were and where the enemy locations were … The aircraft has a data-transfer system. Once they plug that card in they can pull that data up on those maps … You get routes, landing locations, radio frequencies that you need to be on as well as locations of refuel and rearm points.

Rather than purchase new Black Hawks in the future, the US Army plans on a continuing policy of integrating emerging technologies into its UH-60M fleet with the intention of improving their reliability, survivability and maintainability. Relatively recently the US Army has introduced fly-by-wire (FBW) into some of its UH-60M inventory. The aim of FBW is to reduce the pilot workloads so they can spend more time concentrating on what is going on outside their cockpits.

When fitted with an integrated MEDEVAC mission equipment package (MEP) the UH-60M becomes the ultimate aerial ambulance. This configuration also changes the helicopter's designation to HH-60M. With its built-in MEP the HH-60M comes with an electronically-controlled litter system to carry up to six patients. It is also equipped with an onboard oxygen-generating system and electrocardiograph (ECG) machine.

In August 2016, the US Army awarded contracts to two different firms to develop a new-generation gas turbine helicopter engine for its Black Hawk inventory of 2,135 units as well as its current attack helicopter fleet. The US Army is calling for this next-generation gas turbine engine to be 50 per cent more powerful than the existing engines and 25 per cent more fuel-efficient.

Survivability Features

The Black Hawk first saw combat with the US Army during Operation URGENT FURY, the American military invasion of the Caribbean island nation of Grenada in 1983. The unexpected amount of small-arms fire encountered by the Black Hawks during the invasion led to the development of removable Kevlar armour blankets to line the passenger compartment floor when needed. The Black Hawk crews have armoured seats but not the helicopter's passengers.

Other features that make the Black Hawk much more survivable than the Huey include energy-absorbent crew seats and landing gear. The pilot's flight controls are ballistically-hardened and all the helicopter's electrical and hydraulic systems are redundant. The fuel tanks on the Black Hawks are armoured and self-sealing as well as being crash-resistant.

From a 16 November 2007 article published online by the US Army is this quote by a Chief Warrant Officer (CWO). In it he explains a new feature on the UH-60M known as the 'threat indivisibility' system:

> 'If I climb too high, the system will flash red meaning that I'm within range of various bad-guy weapons systems, so it assists me by telling me to fly lower and keeps me out of harm's way,' CWO4 McNeill said. 'The classified system contains known capabilities of friendly and enemy weapons systems. That means we can plan our routes and have a decreased probability of being shot at … that's a huge advantage.'

Due to the threat posed by man-portable, shoulder-fired, low-altitude surface-to-air missiles (MANPADs) such as the Soviet-era SA-7 and its Chinese-made clones, some US Army Black Hawks have been fitted with infrared engine exhaust suppressors as well as infrared jammers. In addition, many have been fitted with radar warning receivers and chaff/flare dispensers.

The Low-Tech Threats

American military involvement in Somalia, Iraq and Afghanistan has shown that the threat from MANPADs to American military helicopters was overstated. This was no doubt due to the addition of the various countermeasure devices fitted to them. Instead, it turned out that the biggest threat to the Black Hawk and other American military helicopters overseas has been small-arms fire and unguided rocket-propelled grenade-launchers (RPGs).

The threat from RPGs was recreated in the 2001 movie titled *Black Hawk Down* that portrayed the downing of two US Army Black Hawks that occurred in Somalia on 3 October 1993. Black Hawks have also been lost in Iraq and Afghanistan to RPGs. As yet there have been no effective countermeasures devised to eliminate this threat, although different types of active protection options have been proposed.

A Foreign Helicopter Enters Service

Filling a new category for the US Army is a modified commercial helicopter from the European consortium of Airbus. The civilian version is labelled the EC-145, with the US Army designation being UH-72A and assigned the name 'Lakota'. The helicopter has a crew of two pilots and room for six passengers. The Lakota was the winner in 2006 of the US Army's Light Utility Helicopter (LUH) programme.

The US Army ordered 345 units of the twin-engine Lakota as the replacement for its remaining inventory of UH-1H Huey helicopters and an existing observation helicopter. Besides supporting US Army training activities in the observer/controller role, it has also been configured as a VIP transport. In the US Army National Guard it performs Homeland Security duties, including counter-drug operations. There is also a MEDEVAC version of the Lakota for use by the US Army and the National Guard.

With the orange bands of a US Army training helicopter is a Bell UH-1A Iroquois. Prior to 1962, it was labelled the HU-1 Iroquois. Like all the versions that followed, it is better known by its popular nickname of the 'Huey'. It was the first production gas turbine engine-powered helicopter to enter American military service in 1959. (*DOD*)

In response to the rising casualty rate of US Army advisors to the ARVN, the US Army deployed its first air ambulance unit in April 1962. It was equipped with the UH-1A Huey seen here. The original plans called for these helicopters to only evacuate sick and wounded American military personnel but this proved unrealistic and they soon began doing the same for the ARVN. (*DOD*)

(**Opposite, above**) Following the UH-1A to South-East Asia in 1963 were the first units of the UH-1B. It was externally almost identical to the 'A' model but was fitted with a more powerful engine and had been lengthened to increase the passenger count. It took over the troop transport role from the CH-21C Shawnee. Pictured here is a restored and operational example during an air show. (*Paul and Loren Hannah*)

(**Above**) The UH-1B with a lengthened fuselage could seat seven armed US Army soldiers as seen in this picture with five on a bench seat and two in front of the bench seat facing back-to-back. If employed in the medical evacuation (MEDEVAC) role there was room for two sitting casualties and three stretcher cases along with a medic. Some were also configured as gunships in South-East Asia. (*Bell*)

(**Opposite, below**) US Army UH-1B transport helicopters are seen in this Vietnam War photograph. Visible on the helicopter in the foreground are small-calibre machine guns on either side of the passenger compartment. They would be manned by the aircraft's crew chiefs. If a landing zone turned out to be too heavily defended, a helicopter formation would normally proceed to a pre-planned alternative landing zone. (*DOD*)

(**Opposite, above**) In this Vietnam War photograph we see US Army UH-1B Huey transports disembarking American soldiers and lifting off as quickly as possible. It was during landing and take-off that the helicopters were most vulnerable. To increase their survivability during follow-on lifts from the same landing zone, Huey pilots always chose different approach and departure routes. (*DOD*)

(**Above**) The USMC needed a modern gas turbine engine-powered helicopter to replace its aging inventory of piston engine-powered Kaman OH-43D Huskies. In 1962, it was decided to acquire a modified version of the US Army UH-1B Huey. In USMC service it was designated the UH-1E, an example of which is pictured here. A feature seen on the UH-1E and not on the UH-1B was the rescue hoist. (*Bell*)

(**Opposite, below**) A restored and operational example of the USMC UH-1E is shown here during an air show in the United States. Like those employed by the US Army, the USMC model of the Huey helicopter performed a wide variety of jobs during the Vietnam War. The most common was the liaison role, followed by the observation role. Some were also configured for the gunship role. (*Paul and Loren Hannah*)

(**Opposite, above**) During the Vietnam War the USAF employed a version of the US Army UH-1B fitted with a more powerful engine that they labelled the UH-1F. Its primary mission was to support a variety of covert operations. Due to their camouflage paint scheme and radio call sign 'Hornet', they were unofficially nicknamed the 'Green Hornets'. Pictured here is a preserved example. (*USAF Museum*)

(**Opposite, below**) Entering into service with the US Army in 1963 was the UH-1D model of the Huey seen here. It featured a new more powerful engine and a longer fuselage to house more passengers. Reflecting its increased length, the large sliding doors on either side of the helicopter's fuselage had two windows rather than the one seen on earlier models of the Huey. (*DOD*)

(**Above**) Terrain conditions in South Vietnam often made it impossible for the pilots of Huey transport helicopters to actually land. In such situations the pilots would hover over a landing spot and their passengers would be forced to jump out of the aircraft as seen in this photograph. This was standard practice in areas of South Vietnam inundated by water or covered with tall jungle grass. (*DOD*)

(**Opposite, above**) The crew chief of a US Army UH-1D takes aim with his machine gun during the Vietnam War. With the introduction of the larger 'D' model of the Huey into the Vietnam War, the remaining units of the UH-1B model were pushed into the gunship role. When the dedicated UH-1C gunship Huey showed up in South-East Asia in 1965, the UH-1B gunships reverted to the troop transport role. (*DOD*)

(**Opposite, below**) Grim-faced US Army soldiers are shown leaving a UH-1D helicopter during the Vietnam War. If the terrain allowed, a typical formation of twelve Huey troop transports would try to arrive and take off from a landing zone at the same time to minimize their exposure to enemy small-arms fire. If all went well, they could disembark their passengers and lift off again within approximately two minutes. (*DOD*)

(**Above**) The last production version of the single-engine Huey helicopter was the UH-1H seen here. Externally it was almost identical to the previous UH-1D. The key external spotting feature of the 'H' model Huey was the deletion of the two vertical VHF homing aerials seen on the fuselage nose of all previous Huey variants. An important internal change to the UH-1H was a more powerful engine. (*DOD*)

(**Opposite, above**) Pictured is a USAF version of the UH-1H being employed in the CSAR role in which it was designated the HH-1H. Unlike fixed-wing aircraft in which the pilot is always on the left and the co-pilot on the right, in the Huey series the arrangement was reversed. Prior to take-off Huey pilots had to perform approximately eighty steps before the aircraft was ready to fly. (*DOD*)

(**Opposite, below**) The last examples of the UH-1H in USAF service were eventually employed as training aircraft, as seen in this picture. In this role they were designated the TH-1H. The USAF also employed an upgraded version of the UH-1H in the MEDEVAC role that they labelled the UH-1V. In the early 1980s the US Army reconfigured approximately 220 units of their UH-1H to the UH-1V standard. (*DOD*)

(**Above**) The USAF UH-1H Huey pictured here can be distinguished from the earlier 'D' model by a small forward-bent metal device located just above the cockpit on the fuselage roof. It is known as the 'pitot tube' and measures helicopter air speed. The large vertical metal tab further back on the fuselage roof is a very high frequency (VHF) radio antenna. (*DOD*)

(**Above**) Looking towards the future, Bell began a company-funded programme in 1965 to design and build a two-engine version of the UH-1D. The USAF liked what they saw and ordered it into production as the UH-IN. It was also taken into service by the USMC as seen here. Visible on the bottom of the UH-1N helicopter fuselage pictured is a small Forward-Looking Infrared (FLIR) camera pod. (*DOD*)

(**Opposite, above**) Pictured during a training exercise is a US Navy UH-1N employed in the CSAR role. Using instruments, the helicopter could be flown in poor weather conditions or during the hours of darkness. Top speed of the helicopter was 203mph with a range of 286 miles. All the US Navy's and USMC UH-1N helicopters were delivered between 1971 and 1979 and both services retired the last of them in 2013. (*DOD*)

(**Opposite, below**) No doubt the last version of the long-lived Huey helicopter series in American military service is the USMC UH-1Y Venom pictured here. Based on the UH-1N, it is better known as the 'Super Huey' within the Corps. In lieu of the standard two-rotor configuration of all the Huey helicopters that preceded it, the Venom has a four-rotor configuration with the blades being all composite. (*DOD*)

(**Opposite, above**) Belonging to the USMC is this UH-1Y Venom shown hovering over the flight deck of a US Navy Landing Platform Helicopter (LPH) ship. The two engines coupled together on this version of the Huey produce a continuous 1,546hp or when required can produce 1,828hp for 2.5 minutes. It has a top speed of 227mph with a maximum range of 150 miles. (*DOD*)

(**Opposite, below**) Despite the ungainly appearance of the USMC UH-1Y Venom pictured compared to the relatively sleek fuselage designs of the Huey helicopters that came before it, its operational parameters far exceeded those of all its predecessors. Note the Forward-Looking Infrared (FLIR) camera under the front of the fuselage and the various weapons with which the aircraft is armed. (*DOD*)

(**Above**) Suppressive fire on the USMC UH-1Y Venom is provided by 2.75in rocket pods fitted to either side of its fuselage as well as machine guns. The example pictured here being operated by a Venom crew chief is a multi-barrel GAU-17/A 7.62mm Gatling-type machine gun. In the US Army it is designated the M134, while in the USAF it is labelled the GAU-2B/A. (*DOD*)

(**Above**) The USMC replacement for the Sikorsky UH-34D was the Boeing CH-46 Sea Knight series helicopter pictured here. When the USMC were formulating the requirements for a UH-34D replacement they mandated that it had to be a helicopter already in development that could be ready for operational testing in 1963. That meant it had to be either an existing Sikorsky or Boeing design with the latter being selected as it showed the most promise in the Corps' opinion. (*DOD*)

(**Opposite, above**) Marine infantrymen are shown disembarking from a CH-46 Sea Knight helicopter during the Vietnam War through the large hydraulically-operated rear ramp. The prototype had first flown in 1961 and was referred to by the company as the Model 107M. The USMC had originally designated it the HRB-1, which translates to helicopter/transport/Boeing. It became the CH-46 Sea Knight in 1962. (*DOD*)

(**Opposite, below**) A downed CH-46 Sea Knight series helicopter in South Vietnam is being prepared by a group of Marines for recovery. The first version of the helicopter in USMC service was the CH-46A. It was powered by two engines labelled the T-58-GE-8B. In theory, they would provide enough power to allow the helicopter to carry seventeen passengers or 4,000lb of internal cargo. (*DOD*)

The CH-46 Sea Knight series helicopter has two 51ft diameter rotors that overlapped each other at the centre of the aircraft's fuselage. To prevent the rotor blades from striking each other they were interconnected by a geared drive shaft that synchronized their rotations which were offset by 60 degrees. The helicopter fuselage is 84ft 4in long and the aircraft height is 16ft 9in. (*DOD*)

Marine infantrymen are shown packed into a CH-46 Sea Knight series helicopter. The cabin compartment is approximately 24ft in length, 6ft high and has a width of 6ft 6in. The initial model of the aircraft was the CH-46A. It had some serious design issues that caused a number of major accidents and resulting loss of life. In response the Corps fielded the upgraded CH-46D in 1967. (*DOD*)

A USMC CH-46 Sea Knight helicopter is shown being directed to land on the flight deck of a US Navy Landing Helicopter Assault (LHA) ship. Once in South Vietnam and subjected to hard use, the accident rate of the CH-46D soon rose. This pushed the Corps to devote 1,000 man hours to overhauling and strengthening the components of each CH-46D from top to bottom, which resolved the aircraft's problems. (*DOD*)

Being flown to a museum is the last operational USMC CH-46 Sea Knight helicopter. Empty, the helicopter weighed 11,585lb. Its maximum take-off weight was 24,300lb. Top speed was 165mph with a range of 184 miles and a service ceiling of 14,000ft. An unofficial nickname for the entire Sea Knight series was the 'Phrog'. *(DOD)*

The standard role for the US Navy's inventory of Sea Knight series helicopters during their long service career was moving supplies from ship to ship as pictured here. The aircraft had an under-fuselage cargo hook and an internal winch to pull pallets of supplies into its cargo bay. Internal cargo could be parachuted out of the helicopter's rear cargo door if required. *(DOD)*

The USMC replacement for the CH-46 Sea Knight series was the tiltrotor MV-22 Osprey pictured on the flight deck of a US Navy Landing Helicopter Assault (LHA) ship. Bell and Boeing had begun work on its development in 1981. The biggest advantages of a tiltrotor aircraft over helicopters are its increased speed in level flight and the ability to reach much higher altitudes. (DOD)

The USMC tiltrotor MV-22 Osprey pictured is in full-forward flight mode. It has a wing span of 84ft 7in, a length of 57ft 4in and a height of 22ft 1in. Cruising speed is 277mph with a service ceiling of 25,000ft. On internal fuel tanks its range is 426 miles. With the external refuelling probe seen on this aircraft, its range is in theory unlimited. (DOD)

(**Opposite, above**) Marine infantrymen are seen here boarding a tiltrotor MV-22 Osprey. It can carry twenty-four seated passengers or thirty-four standing passengers. Empty, the aircraft weighs 33,140lb. When in a short take-off and landing (STOL) the aircraft has a maximum take-off weight of 60,500lb. In a vertical take-off and landing (VTOL) the MV-22 has a maximum take-off weight of 52,870lb. (*DOD*)

(**Opposite, below**) The USMC tiltrotor MV-22 Osprey shown here is armed only with a large-calibre machine gun fired from the open rear ramp of the aircraft by a crew chief. To provide an increased degree of self-protection for the MV-22, a large-calibre remote-control machine-gun kit was developed. It was designed to be fitted under the fuselage of the MV-22 but proved unpopular in combat due to its added weight. (*DOD*)

(**Above**) The Boeing CH-47 Chinook series helicopter seen here during the Vietnam War is pulling an M113 armoured personnel carrier (APC) from a rice field onto a level road. The Chinook first arrived in South-East Asia in 1965. At its peak deployment there were approximately 750 units of the Chinook in service in South-East Asia, which included the original 'A' model and the follow-on 'B' model. (*DOD*)

(**Above**) The CH-47 Chinook series helicopters have always had a large hydraulically-operated rear ramp. It is seen here in the open position on a South Vietnamese mountain top. The Chinook has two large counter-rotating and overlapping rotor blades that are interconnected by a geared drive shaft to prevent them striking each other. Range with internal fuel tanks is 450 miles. (*DOD*)

(**Opposite, above**) The two engines of the Chinook series helicopters are positioned at the upper rear of the aircraft's fuselage, one on either side of the rear rotor pylon. This is in contrast to the now out-of-service CH-46 Sea Knight that had an engine located in both the front and rear rotor pylons. The fuselage of the CH-47 pictured is 50ft 9in in length with a height of 18ft 11in. (*DOD*)

(**Opposite, below**) Somewhere in Afghanistan a CH-47 Chinook series helicopter is shown preparing to pick up a 155mm howitzer as its sling load. The Chinook has three cargo hooks on the bottom of its fuselage. The centre cargo hook is capable of carrying 26,000lb with the other two cargo hooks carrying lesser weight. Empty, the helicopter weighs 24,578lb and has a maximum take-off weight of 50,000lb. (*DOD*)

US Army soldiers disembark from a CH-47 Chinook series helicopter during a training exercise. The Vietnam War era 'A' and 'B' models were replaced by the introduction of a 'D' model in the early 1980s, which in turn was superseded by an 'E' model. One of the changes to the later versions was the replacement of the all-metal rotor blades with composite rotor blades. (DOD)

The Chinook has been progressively upgraded through the decades. Despite the countless design improvements made to the helicopter, one would be hard-pressed to tell the difference between the original CH-47A model and the newest CH-47F version pictured here. The majority of upgrades have been internal rather than external, such as ever more powerful engines and the latest-generation avionics. (DOD)

In this photograph we are looking into the spacious fuselage of a US Army CH-47 Chinook series helicopter. In its latest iteration the helicopter can carry thirty-three seated passengers or twenty-four stretcher cases. In a combat theatre the aircraft is typically armed with three small-calibre machine guns. Top speed of the Chinook is 196mph with a cruising speed of 184mph. The service ceiling is 20,000ft. (*DOD*)

(**Above**) Taking part in the American invasion of the small Caribbean island nation of Grenada in 1983 is a USMC CH-53D helicopter. It and an earlier CH-53A model had both seen service during the Vietnam War. The massive helicopter had a length of 86ft 3in, a height of 24ft 11in and a rotor diameter of 72ft 3in. (*DOD*)

(**Opposite, above**) The USMC CH-53D helicopters were powered by two engines with one located on either side of the forward portion of the aircraft's fuselage as seen in this picture. Together they provided the helicopter with a top speed of 196mph and a range of 540 miles on its internal fuel tanks. Its service ceiling was 21,000ft. Empty it weighed 22,444lb with a maximum take-off weight of 37,400lb. (*DOD*)

(**Opposite, below**) In 1981, the USMC took into service the first units of an upgraded version of the CH-53D Sea Stallion, which was labelled the CH-53E Super Stallion. It had three engines instead of the two found on the earlier Sea Stallion. The third engine is seen in this photograph of a Super Stallion tucked behind the original engine on the left-hand side of the aircraft's upper fuselage. (*DOD*)

(**Opposite, above**) With the third engine the Super Stallion has an empty weight of 33,226lb and a maximum take-off weight of 73,500lb. The top speed is 196mph. External spotting features of the Super Stallion to distinguish it from the earlier Sea Stallion, besides the third engine, are an in-flight refuelling probe and a small FLIR pod projecting out from the lower front fuselage as seen in this picture. (*DOD*)

(**Above**) The USMC CH-53E Super Stallion pictured has seven rotor blades compared to the six on the earlier CH-53A and CH-53D Sea Stallions. Those on the Super Stallion are composites rather than all-metal as were those on earlier versions of the helicopter. A difficult feature to distinguish on the Super Stallion is that its fuselage is 6ft 2in longer than that of the earlier Sea Stallion. (*DOD*)

(**Opposite, below**) As with almost all USMC and US Navy helicopters an important design feature has always been to minimize their footprint on US Navy ships where space is always at a premium. This has meant that rotor blades must have the ability to be folded as seen with this USMC CH-53E Super Stallion on a flight deck elevator of a Landing Helicopter Assault (LHA) ship. (*DOD*)

(**Above**) The intended USMC replacement for the CH-53E Super Stallion is the CH-53K prototype seen here that the Corps has already named the 'King Stallion'. Descended from the Super Stallion, this newest version of the series has more powerful engines that provide almost triple the payload capability. Heavier than its predecessor, it has a narrower fuselage. (*Sikorsky*)

(**Opposite, above**) Flying over downtown Baghdad is the US Army's latest version of the Black Hawk series helicopter designated the UH-60M. Powered by two engines each producing 2,000hp, the aircraft has a top speed of 174mph. There is also an onboard auxiliary power unit for providing the helicopter with electrical power when the two main engines have been switched off. (*DOD*)

(**Opposite, below**) In this picture we are looking at the cockpit of a UH-60M Black Hawk. Visible is the electronic flight information system (EFIS) typically referred to as a 'glass cockpit'. It consists of a digital flight instrument panel which includes liquid crystal displays (LCDs) that present the pilots with a moving map to aid in navigation. The helicopter is also fitted with an automatic direction-finder. (*DOD*)

(**Opposite, above**) A casualty is being carried to a waiting HH-60L MEDEVAC version of the Black Hawk, which is a specialized variant of the series. Note the horizontal arrangement for transporting stretchers in the passenger/cargo compartment of the helicopter. When the need dictates, standard Black Hawks can be configured for the MEDEVAC role by the addition of a medical kit. (*DOD*)

(**Above**) Due to the worldwide commitments of the American military, one of the mandated requirements for the US Army Black Hawk helicopter series was that it be transportable by USAF transports as seen in this picture. The USAF C-130 Hercules can carry one Black Hawk and the C-5 Galaxy six Black Hawks. During the Korean and Vietnam wars helicopters were typically shipped by sea to the theatre of operations. (*DOD*)

(**Opposite, below**) Two US Army UH-60M Black Hawk helicopters are shown preparing to lift off with 105mm howitzers as their sling-load with their crews being carried on board. The UH-60A has a sling-load capacity of 8,000lb and the follow-on 'L' and 'M' models 9,000lb. Maximum take-off weight for the 'A' model was 20,250lb with the latest 'M' model increasing to 22,000lb. (*DOD*)

(**Opposite, above**) On their internal fuel tanks the US Army UH-60 Black Hawk series helicopters have an approximate range of 370 miles. With the addition of stub wings attached to either side of the aircraft's upper fuselage and external fuel tanks as seen in this picture, Black Hawks can reach a distance of almost 1,400 miles. There is a de-icing system for the rotor blades. (*DOD*)

(**Above**) A US Army UH-60M Black Hawk is shown preparing to lift off with a 4 × 4 Humvee. The cockpit cabin doors on either side of the aircraft can be jettisoned by the pilots if need be and the windows on the helicopter sliding cargo door can be pushed out in case of a crash. The fuel tanks are crashworthy, as are the seats for both the pilots. (*DOD*)

(**Opposite, below**) The US Army UH-60M Black Hawk pictured here has just lifted off. The four rotor blades on the helicopter are constructed of a composite and glass-reinforced plastic mixture, which is wrapped around a titanium spar. The spar is the main longitudinal member of the rotor blade. The leading edge of the rotors is sheathed with nickel to protect them when striking any external object. (*DOD*)

(**Above**) The first foreign-designed helicopter to be taken into service by the US Army is the UH-72A Lakota of which two are pictured here. It is a variant of the commercial Airbus helicopter labelled the EC-145 and is built under licence in the United States. Empty, the aircraft weighs 3,951lb and has a maximum take-off weight of 7,903lb. (*DOD*)

(**Opposite, above**) Visible in this picture taken inside the cockpit of a US Army UH-72A Lakota is the aircraft's electronic flight information system (EFIS). The helicopter has a top speed of 167mph and a cruising speed of 153mph. It has a range of 426 miles on its internal fuel tanks and a service ceiling of 13,480ft. An add-on Forward-Looking Infrared (FLIR) system can be fitted to the helicopter. (*DOD*)

(**Opposite, below**) Pictured is the MEDEVAC model of the US Army UH-72A Lakota. The helicopter has a length of 42ft 7in and is 11ft 9in in height. In 2013 the American Congress questioned why the US Army had not considered a weapon-armed version. The explanation was cost and the matter was dropped. (*DOD*)

Chapter Three

Gunships and Attack Helicopters

As soon as the first helicopter entered the American military inventory, there were individuals trying to figure out how to turn it into a weapons platform. A number of experiments were conducted by the American military following the Second World War on the possibility of creating a helicopter gunship. However, it was the French army that took the next big step and began turning their American-made and non-American-made helicopters into gunships for use during the Algerian War (1954–62).

Inspired by what the French army was doing with its gunships, the US Army pursued its own line of development. The biggest limiting factor was the poor performance parameters of the existing piston-engine-powered helicopters. With the introduction of the more powerful gas turbine engine-powered prototype Huey in the late 1950s, some in the US Army felt they finally had a helicopter that would be suitable for use as a gunship.

Huey Gunships

In 1960, the US Army began testing a small number of production UH-1As and prototypes of the follow-on UH-1B as potential gunship platforms. The armament tested on these early-model Huey helicopters included machine guns of varying calibre, unguided rockets, 20mm cannons and guided anti-tank missiles. The latter reflected the threat in Western Europe posed by thousands of Soviet and Warsaw Pact tanks in Eastern Europe.

Eventually the army decided that the best weapon for the more powerful UH-1B was a combination of 7.62mm machine guns and 2.75in (70mm) unguided rockets. These were affixed to structural attachment fittings (referred to as hard points) on either side of the helicopter's fuselage. The UH-1A had lacked these factory hard points so the machine-gun and rocket pods had been attached to the helicopters' landing-skids.

From a US Army publication titled *Seven Firefights in Vietnam*, the section referred to as the 'Gun Ship Mission', appears this extract describing the weapon arrangement on a Huey gunship in a 1968 engagement:

Davis' helicopter mounted the XM16 weapons system, consisting of two externally mounted 7.62mm M60CA1 machine guns ('flexguns') and fourteen 2.75-inch folding-fin aerial rockets, seven on each side of the ship … The rockets could be fired singly, in pairs, or in salvos from their cylindrical pods to a maximum effective range of 2,500 meters for area targets. They were most effective against point targets at 200–500 meters.

Into Operational Service

A quantity of UH-1As and UH-1Bs were sent to South Vietnam in 1962 as gunships. Whereas the 'A' model Huey helicopters were fitted with locally-fabricated weapon hard points, the 'B' model came with factory-installed weapon hard points. The primary job of both these ad hoc gunships was escorting US Army and USMC helicopter troop transports.

Combat action in South Vietnam soon showed that when troop transport helicopters were escorted by helicopter gunships, the efficiency of the enemy anti-aircraft fire dropped by as much as 25 per cent. The downside was the fact that the helicopter gunships typically flew at no more than 100 to 200ft above the ground in support of these missions and took the brunt of enemy anti-aircraft fire.

A problem with employing the UH-1B in the gunship role and by default the UH-1A appears in this extract from a US Army publication titled *Vietnam Studies: Airmobility 1961–1971* by Lieutenant General John J. Tolson (retired):

> The UH-1B was not designed for an armed configuration and the weight of the armament system reduced the maneuverability of the aircraft and induced sufficient drag to lower the maximum speed to approximately 80 knots [92mph]. As a consequence, the armed helicopters could not overtake the airmobile force if they left the formation to attack targets en route. The early armed UH-1Bs did an outstanding job in proving the concept of the armed helicopters, but they also pointed out many deficiencies that the Army would correct in later versions.

In 1972, two US Army UH-1B gunships armed with the new Tube-launched, Optically-tracked, Wire-guided (TOW) anti-tank missiles were shipped to South Vietnam. On arrival they were pressed into service in an effort to repel invading North Vietnamese army tanks. The 162 TOW missiles fired between 1972 and 1973 destroyed 53 vehicles: 27 tanks, 21 trucks and 5 armoured personnel carriers. Additionally the missiles knocked out a variety of other enemy weapons such as anti-aircraft guns.

USMC Huey Gunships

The USMC, as already mentioned, took into service modified versions of the UH-1B and a later model, both of which were designated the UH-1E. With the failure of the

HUS-1/UH-34D as a gunship, the USMC decided that the UH-1E was the next best choice. The first so-modified helicopter arrived in South Vietnam in 1964. The USMC fixed-wing aircraft leadership greatly resisted this development as they felt it would be subverting their long-time role.

Rather than using the armament kits designed and built for the US Army's Huey gunships, the USMC designed and built its own armament kits for the UH-1Es that the Corps converted into gunships. However, they did attach them to the standard hard points on Huey models starting with the US Army's UH-1B. The problem with employing the UH-1E as a gunship was that it was therefore unavailable for a whole host of roles the USMC felt were just as important, such as MEDEVAC.

US Navy Huey Gunships

In 1965 the US Navy formed a riverine force known as the 'Brown Water Navy' whose mission was to patrol South Vietnam's Mekong Delta region that is located in the south-eastern portion of the country. As neither the US Army nor the USAF was able to provide sufficient aerial support, the US Navy borrowed twenty-two of the US Army's UH-1B gunships beginning in 1967. These were crewed by US Navy personnel and referred to as the 'Seawolves'.

From a US Navy historical publication titled *War in the Shallows: US Navy Coastal and Riverine Warfare in Vietnam 1965–1968* written by John Darrell Sherwood is this extract describing the role played by the Seawolves:

> From its inception the Seawolves were designed as a quick-reaction force. Two ship formations would stand alert for 24-hour shifts and respond to close air support requests up to 50 miles away from their base. Requests could come at any time of day or night, in fair weather or foul. Some missions lasted no longer than five minutes, and others could stretch on for over an hour. As soon as a unit completed a mission, all crew members (including the pilot and co-pilot) worked furiously to reload and refuel the aircraft, sometimes in a 'hot' mode with the engine running.

Originally armed with 7.62mm machine-gun and 2.75in rocket-launcher pods, some of the US Navy helicopter gunships were eventually armed with 12.7mm machine guns. This was because their larger and more powerful projectiles were better able to punch through thick foliage. Multi-barrel 7.62mm mini-guns also became popular on the Seawolves.

Within the Mekong Delta region the Seawolves operated from Second World War-vintage US Navy Landing Ship, Tanks (LSTs) with two assigned to each vessel. By the time the Seawolves were stood down in 1972, they had flown over 100,000 combat sorties and taken a heavy toll on the enemy but in the process had 44 flight crewmen killed and 200 wounded.

Model 'C' Huey

To overcome the problems encountered with the underpowered UH-1A and UH-1B Huey helicopters employed in the gunship role, the US Army ordered into production 766 units of a modified 'B' model Huey with a more powerful engine and longer rotor blades to improve lift. It was assigned the designation UH-1C and was also known as the 'Charlie' model based on the American military radio alphabet code word.

The UH-1C Huey was a dedicated gunship, and was intended to serve until such time as a new ground-up design gunship could be placed into service. The first examples would show up in South Vietnam in 1965 as a replacement for the UH-1B Huey gunships.

The UH-1C Huey had a crew of four and could carry six seated passengers. Besides the standard machine-gun and rocket armament kits, they were also armed with a 40mm automatic grenade-launcher. The latter was mounted inside a travers-able pod fitted in the nose of the aircraft's fuselage.

Night-Fighting Huey Gunships

To deny the enemy the cover of night during the Vietnam War, the US Army employed various methods. At first it was simply using helicopter flare ships, which then progressed to mounting bright lights on UH-1D Huey helicopters that were shadowed by a blacked-out UH-1C Huey gunship that waited to engage any targets identified by the light ship.

As an experiment, five UH-1Cs had their nose-mounted 40mm grenade-launchers replaced by an electro-optical image intensifier system. Four were shipped to South Vietnam and unofficially nicknamed 'Batships'. Positive results with the Batships led to thirty-six units of the UH-1C being fitted with a more powerful engine and labelled the UH-1M.

With more weight-carrying ability, the UH-1Ms were fitted with both an electro-optical image intensifier system and a Low Light Level Television (LLLTV) system. They arrived in South-East Asia in 1969 and remained until the end of American military involvement in 1973.

Both the UH-1D and UH-1H Huey models would be armed on occasion with a variety of weapons. However, they were generally reserved as troop transports during the Vietnam War.

Chinook Gunships and Bombers

As a test, Boeing Vertol converted four 'B' model Chinooks into gunships. Three were sent to South Vietnam where they quickly received the unofficial nickname of the 'Go-Go Birds'. Armament consisted of two 20mm cannons with one mounted on either side of the fuselage, five small or large-calibre machine guns and at least one or more 40mm grenade-launchers. One was mounted in a rotating gun pod in the nose of the aircraft and aimed and fired by the co-pilot.

The three Go-Go Birds were lost in South Vietnam. The first was destroyed on the ground when it crashed into another helicopter while taxiing. The second was shot down by one of its own 20mm cannons when the weapon became loose and pivoted upwards in its gun mount and destroyed the helicopter's own rotor system. The third was destroyed in combat.

The loss of three of the four Go-Go Birds, the large amount of ground support needed to keep these specialized gunships functioning properly and the unwillingness of US Army units in South-East Asia to give up these vital helicopters in the transport role brought the programme to an end.

Reflecting the never-ending inventiveness of soldiers in theatres of combat, the US Army C-47 Chinook was pushed into the unbelievable role of a bomber during its time in South-East Asia. Rather than high-explosive (HE) bombs, a few Chinooks were fitted with racks inside their fuselage in which tear gas or napalm drums would be stored. When hovering over a known enemy-held location, the crew chiefs would push these drums off the lowered rear ramp of the helicopter to detonate upon impact.

State-of-the-Art Attack Helicopter

In the early 1960s, the US Army began looking for the 'ultimate' dedicated gunship. It was intended as the replacement for the interim 'B' and 'C' model Huey gunships and would feature all the latest technology. Both Sikorsky and Lockheed submitted design proposals for consideration. In 1965, the US Army announced that they preferred the Lockheed design, which the firm labelled the CL-840.

In 1966, the US Army awarded Lockheed a contract to build ten prototypes of their CL-840 for testing. These were assigned the designation AH-56A. The prefix letter 'A' in the aircraft's designation stood for attack. In 1967, the AH-56A acquired the official nickname 'Cheyenne'.

The Cheyenne was to have an under-fuselage turret that could be armed with anything from a 40m grenade-launcher to a 30mm cannon. Also part of the aircraft's armament mix would have been both 2.75in rockets and guided anti-tank missiles.

In 1967, the US Army announced that they were going to order the first 375 units of the Cheyenne with the expectation that 1,000 units would eventually be taken into service. The US Army's rush to field the Cheyenne was being driven by combat experience in South Vietnam. Unfortunately, the rising cost of the war in South-East Asia was matched by the ever-increasing costs of the very complex Cheyenne.

Another factor weighing against the Cheyenne was its inability to fly nap-of-the-earth (NOE), taking advantage of terrain-masking. This would soon become a crucial issue as the Soviet army was greatly improving its anti-aircraft defences against high-flying attack helicopters of the 1960s like the Cheyenne. This, and a host of other issues, led to the Cheyenne's cancellation in 1969.

A Solution Appears

Bell Helicopter anticipated the US Army's problems with the Cheyenne and offered a cost-effective alternative. They proposed an interim off-the-shelf attack helicopter based on proven UH-1-series Huey helicopter components. Bell referred to their new attack helicopter design as the Model 209 and named it the 'Huey Cobra'. The US Army liked what they saw and ordered it into production in 1966 as the AH-1G with 1,100 units delivered between 1967 and 1973.

The army would officially nickname the AH-1G the 'Cobra', making it the first US Army helicopter since the introduction of the H-19 Chickasaw in the early 1950s to not be assigned a Native American or woodland animal name. The Cobra was intended as a stop-gap attack helicopter in anticipation of delivery of the Cheyenne. It was unofficially nicknamed the 'Snake' by some who flew it due to its narrow fuselage.

In an article titled 'Cobra' that appeared in the August 1969 issue of *US Army Aviation Digest* magazine, the author, Captain William H. Meeler, discussed the new attack helicopter:

> Except for the loss of the crew chief and [door] gunner, it is the gun pilot's dream. It will fly faster, carry more of a payload and stay in the area of operation longer than any other gunship. It is very sleek with a 36-inch wide fuselage which employs tandem seating, a new concept in Army helicopters ... The smooth, sleek lines of the Cobra with the [1,400hp] engine enable the aircraft to obtain speeds of 190 knots [219mph] in a firing pass.

Cruising speed of the Cobra was 166mph. Unlike the Cheyenne, it could fly NOE for short periods of time. Compared to the Huey gunships that came before it, the Cobra was well-protected. Besides the provision of armoured seats for the pilot and gunner/co-pilot, many of the helicopter's vital components were protected by armour. Combat in South-East Asia clearly showed that it was the pilots in the Cobra that were the most vulnerable part of the aircraft as their canopies were made of non-ballistic plastic.

Into the Fray

The early-production Cobras had a chin turret armed with a single multi-barrel Gatling-type 7.62mm machine gun designated the M134 and labelled the 'mini-gun'. Later-production units had a chin turret armed with a 40mm grenade-launcher and a mini-gun.

There was storage on the AH-1G for 4,000 of the 7.62mm rounds and between 200 and 300 rounds for the grenade-launcher. Depending on mission requirements or crew preference, there could be two mini-guns fitted in the chin turret or two 40mm grenade-launchers.

On the Cobra's two external hard points, referred to as 'stub wings', 2.75in rocket pods or mini-gun pods could be fitted. On the left-hand-side stub wing a three-barrel 20mm cannon pod designated the XM-35 could also be fitted.

The 2.75in unguided rockets employed at the time on the Cobra and all the ad hoc gunships that came before it were referred to in the American military as Folding-Fin Aerial Rockets (FFARs). There were no guided anti-tank missiles available for the Cobra during its time in South-East Asia.

In this extract from a US Army publication, *Vietnam Studies: Airmobility 1961–1971* by Lieutenant General John J. Tolson (retired), is this description on how the Cobra crews dealt with North Vietnamese Army PT-76 light tanks in 1971:

> Initially, anti-tank rockets were not available: engagement was made with ordnance on hand. Upon sighting a tank the Cobras would initiate contact at maximum range with 2.75-inch flechette rockets. This served to wipe personnel off the vehicles and their immediate proximity. As the gun run continued, the AH-1G pilots would begin firing a mixture of high-explosive and white phosphorous rockets, breaking off the run at approximately 500 meters [546 yards] and indeed, often overflying the target.

Attacking the North Vietnamese tanks with the Cobra's XM-35 20mm cannon pod met with mixed success as there were no armour-piercing (AP) 20mm rounds available. Eventually 2.75in anti-tank rockets did become available. However, there arose the problem of firing them accurately. To do so required the Cobra to be within 547 to 1,094 yards of the enemy tanks being targeted. This put them within range of the tank's 12.7mm anti-aircraft guns and other enemy small-arms weaponry.

New enemy aircraft weapons that appeared late in the Vietnam War, such as MANPADs in 1970, were forcing the Cobra pilots to fly lower to the ground than they had before. This exposed them to heavy small-arms fire, which took its toll. A total of 270 were lost during the Vietnam War, with ten of those attributed to MANPADs.

Improved US Army Cobras

Upon the conclusion of the Vietnam War, the US Army once again turned its attention to Western Europe. There the threat of the Soviet army's massive tank inventory remained. This pushed the US Army to field 101 units of a slightly modified version of the AH-1G Cobra that was armed with the TOW anti-tank missile system. That model was designated as the AH-1Q. Unfortunately, it retained the same 1,400hp engine of its predecessor, which left it underpowered with the full complement of eight TOW missiles aboard.

To solve the issue with the AH-1Q being underpowered, the US Army had Bell Helicopter develop an upgraded version of the AH-1G powered by a 1,800hp engine. It now had enough lifting power to carry a full complement of eight TOW missiles. This up-powered AH-1G was given the designation AH-1S with 290 units delivered: 92 were rebuilt AH-1Qs and the other 198 were rebuilt AH-1Gs.

Despite these upgrades, the AH-1S had serious limitations that are mentioned in the Department of the Army Historical Summary of 1987:

> The Cobra [AH-1S] is not regarded as optimally effective because it fires the wire-guided TOW missile. Wire guidance requires the helicopter to remain exposed to hostile fire while guiding the missile to the designated target. This also limits the Cobra to performing only during daylight and in fair weather.

Using the original AH-1S as a base, Bell continually added progressively-improved high-technology features to the helicopter's design, resulting in sub-variants. Beginning in 1988, they were assigned their own designations. This resulted in the AH-1P and the AH-1E model designations. There were 100 units of the former delivered to the US Army beginning in 1977 and 98 units of the latter beginning in 1978.

The last model of the Cobra series was designated the AH-1F and, unlike all the previous models, had the ability to operate in some types of adverse weather conditions. Some 387 units of the 'F' model Cobra consisted of rebuilt 'G' model Cobras, with 143 being new-built units. The US Army pulled its last AH-1F Cobra from service in 1999 due to the introduction of a new attack helicopter.

USMC Cobras

USMC interest in the US Army Cobra attack helicopters prompted them to take thirty-eight units of the 'G' model Cobra into service in 1969. These were employed by the USMC during the Vietnam War. The USMC appreciated the enhanced capabilities of the AH-1G Cobra over their UH-1E gunships. However, the USMC needed a version optimized for shipboard use.

What the USMC eventually took into service starting in 1971 was the first of 118 units of the AH-1J that was officially nicknamed the 'Sea Cobra'. It was powered by two coupled engines that each produced 900hp. It had a chin turret armed with the three-barrel XM197 20mm cannon. The AH-1J Sea Cobra was also typically armed with 2.75in rocket pods.

The reason that the USMC wanted their Sea Cobra to have two engines rather than the single engine on the US Army AH-1Gs appears in this passage from an historical monograph titled *Marines and Helicopters 1962–1973* written by Lieutenant Colonel William R. Fails (retired):

> Another factor, which the Army did not have to face, was that the Marine Corps mission was based on amphibious landings. At sea, in an aircraft with only one

engine, a malfunction almost invariably led to the loss of the helicopter and often some of the crew. Recent experience with the twin-powered CH-53 [Sea Stallion] and CH-46 [Sea Knight] had proved that with two engines, if one malfunctioned, not only could the crew be saved, but often the aircraft, too.

Four units of the USMC AH-1J were sent to South Vietnam for combat testing in 1971. After a four-month trial period the testing was considered a success, as the second engine of the 'J' model Cobra allowed them to carry a much larger weapon load than the single-engine 'G' model Cobra. This reaffirmed the USMC belief in the benefits of a twin-engine installation.

New Models Appear

The AH-1J Sea Cobra was not equipped to handle the TOW anti-tank missile system. That feature was added to the subsequent redesigned and upgraded AH-1T version that entered USMC service beginning in 1979. The AT-1T, or 'Improved Sea Cobra', eventually evolved into the AH-1W version that was officially nicknamed the 'Super Cobra' or unofficially the 'Whiskey Cobra'.

Entering service in 1986, the AH-1W was powered by two coupled engines that each produced 1,690hp. In total 222 units entered USMC service. The AH-1W came with full night-fighting capability with the Night Targeting System (NTS). The fire-control system has a Heads-Up-Display (HUD) with Doppler navigator, which helps pilots to seek and engage targets with different weapons.

In an occasional paper by the USMC Historical Center titled *23 Days to Baghdad* by Colonel Patricia D. Saint (retired) appears this passage describing the contributions made during the initial stage of Operation IRAQI FREEDOM in 2003 by AH-1W attack helicopters:

> Typically, Cobra aircrews took 30–45 minutes to fire their missiles before they flew a short distance, usually less than 10 minutes, to quickly refuel and rearm. Flying at altitudes as low as 100 feet and at speeds of 80–120 knots [92–138mph], aviators destroyed a mix of well-defended Iraqi targets, including tanks, armed vehicles, mortar positions, and recoilless rifles. A typical Cobra ordnance load included 2.75-inch Hydra 70 rockets, AGM-114 Hellfire missiles, and an M197 20mm cannon.

The Newest Version of an Old Favourite

The latest attack helicopter version of the Cobra in USMC service is designated the AH-1Z and officially nicknamed the 'Viper'. Entering into service in 2003 and typically referred to unofficially as the 'Zula Cobra', these are upgraded AH-1W gunships. A new bearing-less four-bladed foldable rotor system on the AH-1Z has greatly increased its payload and speed. It is powered by the same two engines found on the UH-1Y Venom and shares many of the same components.

The AH-1Z has energy-absorbing landing skids with the flight crew having armoured energy-reducing crashworthy seats. Like the AH-1W, the 'Z' model fuselage is designed to resist small-arms projectiles, with rotor blades that can withstand the impact of 23mm projectiles. In addition, the helicopter is fitted with warning systems to alert the flight crew when they are being targeted by either radar or laser illuminators.

The AH-1Z has an impressive weaponry array that can include up to sixteen Hellfire guided missiles that are equally effective against targets on land such as tanks or surface vessels. Other weapons include 2.75in unguided rocket pods and air-to-air infrared (IR) guided missiles for engaging enemy helicopters or fixed-wing aircraft. Non-weapon items that can be carried include nighttime illumination flares and 100-gallon external fuel tanks.

Let Us Keep Trying

The cancellation of the Cheyenne in 1969 pushed the US Army in 1972 to once again search for the ultimate attack helicopter. It compiled a list of design requirements under a programme titled 'The Advanced Attack Helicopter' (AAH). Unlike the Cheyenne, the design sought was supposed to be able to fly NOE and be tough enough to withstand hits by both Soviet 12.7mm and 23mm rounds.

Five companies submitted their proposed twin-engine attack helicopter designs to the US Army for consideration. Two companies were asked to provide prototypes for testing in 1973. In 1976, the service announced that it had selected the Hughes Aircraft Company submission, labelled the Model 77, and designated it the AH-64A. In 1984, Hughes Helicopters was acquired by McDonnell Douglas.

The AH-64A was officially assigned the nickname 'Apache' in 1981. Authorization for full production of the helicopter did not occur until 1982 with the first production unit coming off the factory floor the following year. The US Army ordered approximately 800 units of the 'A' model Apache, with the first examples entering operational service in 1986.

Apache Weaponry

The armament suite of the AH-64A Apache consisted of three weapons. The first is the M230 30mm cannon, with the second and third mounted on the helicopter's external hard points and including unguided 2.75in rocket pods or long-range Hellfire guided anti-tank missiles. Of the various weapons carried into combat by the AH-64A, the most important was the original Hellfire guided missile now labelled the AGM-114 and named the 'Basic Hellfire'.

The development of what became the original Hellfire began in 1974 with initial fielding taking place in 1982. A description of the Hellfire on the AH-64A appeared in a December 1985 article in *US Army Aviation Digest* magazine titled 'AH-64

Apache'. It was written by the helicopter's then programme manager Major General Charles F. Drenz:

> The Apache has the capability to carry a maximum of 16 Hellfires for anti-armor missions. Each missile has a [semi-active] laser seeker that homes in on laser spot energy reflected by a designated target. Its shaped charge warhead attacks a tank in its upper area where it is most vulnerable. Combined with the laser designators of the TADS, or other remote designators, Hellfire provides an anti-armor punch at greater stand-off ranges than is achievable by TOW.

All the weapons fitted to the AH-64A Apache were controlled by the onboard Target Acquisition Designation System (TADS), which was combined with a Pilot Night Vision System (PNVS). The TADS assembly located at the very front of the helicopter's fuselage contained a variety of stabilized electro-optical sensors, a laser range-finder and a laser designator. The back-up for the TADS was provided by the Integrated Helmet and Display Sight System (IHADSS) worn by the pilot and gunner/co-pilot, which was connected to the helicopter's Forward-Looking Infrared (FLIR) system.

New Model Apache

To take advantage of the latest technology, in 1998 the US Army began fielding a new version of the Apache, designated the AH-64D. It was built by Boeing, which took over McDonnell Douglas in 1997. All 'D' model Apaches were rebuilds of 'A' model Apaches. The last AH-64A was pulled from service in 2012 for rebuilding into an AH-64D.

Unlike the AH-64A model with analogue instrument panels for its two-man crew, the 'D' model had a digital multi-function instrument panel commonly referred to as a 'glass cockpit'. When fitted with a mast-mounted removable Fire-Control Radar (FCR) unit named the 'Longbow', the AH-64D becomes the AH-64D Longbow Apache (LBA). From a Lockheed Martin marketing release appears this extract, which describes the capabilities of the Longbow FCR:

> The Longbow FCR has a very low probability of intercept [jamming]. It rapidly and automatically searches, detects, locates, classifies, and prioritizes multiple moving and stationary targets on land, water and in the air in all weather and battlefield conditions from stand-off ranges. Target coordinates are auto-matically available to other sensors and weapons for target confirmation, rapid engagement, and reduced fratricide.

The Longbow FCR allows the AH-64D Apache so fitted to employ a fire-and-forget version of the Hellfire with an inertial guidance system. It was designated the AGM-114L and officially nicknamed the 'Longbow Hellfire'.

AH-64D Apache Upgrade Feature

The first Modernized TADS (M-TADS/PNVS) units, referred to as the 'Apache Arrowhead' by the manufacturer, began appearing on the AH-64D fleet in 2005. What the M-TADS/PNVS brought to the Apache is described in this extract from an online US Army article dated 3 March 2009:

> The new M-TADS/PNVS system allows for better targeting and tracking, giving the crew a better chance at identifying friendly forces from the enemy. It makes the ground fighter feel safer when these aircraft are in the air giving them support. It has also improved the night vision FLIR, allowing the pilots better vision when flying at night and has made flight safer for the crew because they are able to see better and identify hazards easier.

The Latest Version of the Apache

Beginning in 2012, the US Army began replacing the AH-64D with the AH-64E model officially nicknamed the 'Guardian'. Of the 690 units ordered, the majority will be rebuilt units of the AH-64D with final delivery to be completed by 2025. What the Guardian brings to the battlefield appears in this passage from a 12 March 2013 US Army online article:

> The newest model of the heavily-armed, twin engine helicopter … integrates several new technologies such as more powerful, fuel-efficient engines, improved rotor blade technology and advanced electronics. The upgrades significantly increase aircraft reliability and sustainability by improving the Apache's range, performance, and maneuverability … It has a combat speed of around 189mph, about 23mph faster than the Longbow. The Guardian will also turn faster and tighter, making it significantly more difficult for the enemy to outmaneuver the aircraft.

The pilots of the Guardian also have the option to control nearby Unmanned Aerial Vehicles (UAVs), allowing them to view the UAV camera feeds, adjust their flight path when required and launch its Hellfire missiles at targets identified by the UAVs. To share this information the Guardian is also fitted with the Link 16 Tactical Data Link System. It is a secure joint, wireless network-in-the-sky, allowing the critical information to be disseminated in real time to other friendly aircraft as well as ground and sea platforms.

On a restored UH-1B Huey we see the right-hand portion of the M6 armament sub-system kit consisting of four (quad) small-calibre 7.62mm machine guns. There would be an identical arrangement on the other side of the aircraft with two additional machine guns. The 2.75in rocket tube arrangement was an add-on feature made in South Vietnam to beef up the helicopter's firepower. *(Paul and Loren Hannah)*

From a manual is this illustration of some of the various components that made up the M6 armament sub-system as fitted to the 'B' and 'C' models of the Huey. The 7.62mm M60C machine guns were fed by long flexible metal chutes connected to ammunition boxes as seen in this illustration. An electric motor allowed the pilot to slew the machine guns in various directions. *(DOD)*

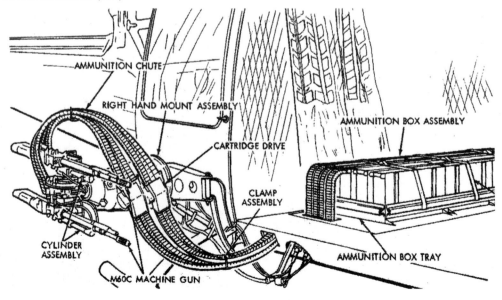

Taking aim with his M6 armament sub-system sighting system is a US Navy pilot of a UH-1B Huey gunship during the Vietnam War. The sighting system allowed the pilot to see a projectile reticle image that he could line up with his intended target. He could slew his machine guns 70 degrees outboard, 10 degrees upward and 85 degrees downward. (DOD)

In this Vietnam War vintage picture of a UH-1B Huey we can see two of the four 7.62mm M60C machine guns that made up the M6 armament sub-system kit. Added to the armament kit during the early part of the Vietnam War was the MA-2 rocket system pod seen here with 2.75in rockets, an arrangement duplicated on the other side of the helicopter. (DOD)

(**Opposite, above**) In this UH-1B Huey gunship the two-part sighting system for the onboard weapons in front of the pilot and co-pilot are visible. They are both suspended from the cockpit ceiling by flexible metal frameworks. The one on the left controls the slewing movement of the four machine guns of the M6 armament sub-system, while the other was normally employed to aim and fire the non-slewing 2.75in rockets. (*DOD*)

(**Above**) The early 2.75in rocket pods attached to Huey gunships during the Vietnam War were improvised and locally fabricated. The first 2.75in rocket pod built to US Army requirements was the seven-tube M157 seen here attached to a UH-1B gunship M6 armament sub-system kit. With these weapons combined it became the M16 armament sub-system kit. (*DOD*)

(**Opposite, below**) A US Navy UH-1B Huey gunship is shown launching a 2.75in rocket during the Vietnam War. The 2.75in rocket being fired was originally developed in the late 1940s by the USAF as an air-to-air weapon and was officially the Mk 4 Folding-Fin Aerial Rocket and nicknamed the 'Mighty Mouse'. It was modified for use during the Vietnam War by the other services as an air-to-ground weapon. (*DOD*)

(**Above**) The replacement for the M16 armament sub-system kit was the M21 armament sub-system kit seen here. It consisted of two six-barrel 7.62mm M134 mini-guns, one on either side of a Huey gunship fuselage. As with its predecessor, two 2.75in rocket-launcher pods were typically added. The rocket pod pictured was designated the M158. (*DOD*)

(**Opposite, above**) The M21 armament sub-system kit was attached via a pylon extension to the M157 universal mount, both of which are visible in this picture. The universal mount was in turn affixed to structural attachment fittings on either side of a UH-1B or later Huey helicopter lower fuselages. These structural attachment fittings are commonly referred to as 'hard points' on both helicopters and fixed-wing aircraft. (*DOD*)

(**Opposite, below**) To see just how much firepower could be added to the UH-1B Huey gunship, the US Army experimentally armed the aircraft with two 20mm M24A1 cannons, one of which is seen here. In South Vietnam it was encased in an aerodynamic-shaped plastic pod to reduce drag. Within the electrically-powered pod were 600 rounds of ammunition. It was designated the XM-31 but did not see widespread employment. (*DOD*)

(**Above**) Another attempt to arm the UH-1B Huey with the 20mm M24A1 cannon resulted in the experimental arrangement seen here. The US Army also tried mounting the three-barrel M61 Vulcan Gatling-type 20mm cannon in the UH-1B. However, the recoil forces generated proved to be more than the helicopter's airframe could tolerate and the experiment was cancelled. (*DOD*)

(**Opposite, above**) An early-war twenty-four-tube 2.75in rocket armament pod designated the XM3 is seen here. It is fitted to a US Army UH-1B Huey gunship with the matching example seen on the other side of the helicopter. The rockets had to be fired from both pods at the same time, otherwise the aircraft would become unbalanced in flight due to the shift in weight. (*DOD*)

(**Opposite, above**) Pictured is the interim UH-1C model Huey gunship. It was placed into service as a bridge between the underpowered UH-1B gunships seeing service in South-East Asia and the advent of a dedicated helicopter gunship. It is armed with the XM-3 rocket system and the M5 armament sub-system in the lower front fuselage nose of the aircraft shown. (*DOD*)

An M5 armament sub-system pod is shown here mounted in the fuselage nose of a UH-1C Huey gunship. It was armed with a 40mm air-cooled, electrically-powered 40mm grenade-launcher. The traversable pod could be turned 60 degrees left or right and elevated upward 15 degrees and downward 35 degrees. It was capable of firing 220 to 240 rounds per minute. (*DOD*)

In the markings of the Army of the Republic of Vietnam (ARVN) is an American-supplied UH-1H model Huey. As is visible in the picture, it has been configured as a gunship. It is armed with the seven-tube 2.75in rocket-launcher pod labelled the M157 and a manually-operated version of the 7.62mm six-barrel M134 mini-gun. (DOD)

Mounted on the fuselage of a CH-47A Chinook gunship in South Vietnam are both a 20mm M24A cannon and the nineteen-shot XM159 rocket-launcher pod. The latter was also fitted to Huey gunships. Besides the 20mm cannon and rocket pods the Chinook gunships, nicknamed 'Go-Go Birds' or 'Guns a Go-Go', had an M5 armament sub-system pod mounted in the lower front fuselage nose. (DOD)

(**Opposite, above**) Pictured on display at a US Army museum is one of the ten prototypes built of the Lockheed AH-56A Cheyenne for testing by the US Army. To reduce drag and improve its speed, both the two wheels of the main landing gear and the tail wheel were retractable as is visible in this photograph. Besides 2.75in rockets, the aircraft could carry on its stub wings up to sixteen Tube-launched, Optically-tracked, Wire-guided (TOW) anti-tank missiles. (*Paul and Loren Hannah*)

(**Opposite, below**) Early-production units of the AH-1G Huey Cobra built up to 1966 had landing lights mounted in the nose of the fuselage as seen in this picture. Later-production units of the helicopter came with retractable landing lights located in the fuselage behind the weapon-armed chin turret. The Huey Cobra pictured here has an early chin turret armed only with a single M134 7.62mm mini-gun. (*Bell*)

(**Above**) The landing lights in the nose of the AH-1G Huey Cobra seen here in South Vietnam and the single M134 7.62mm mini-gun in the TAT-102A chin turret mark it as an early-production unit. On the outer extremity of the aircraft's right-hand-side stub wing is a seven-shot M159 2.75in rocket-launcher pod. Inboard of that rocket pod is the much larger 7.62mm mini-gun M18A1 gun pod that proved much more reliable in service than the M134 7.62mm mini-gun in the helicopter's chin turret. (*DOD*)

(**Above**) An external identification feature of early-production units of the AH-1G Huey Cobra was the tail rotor mounted on the left-hand side of the tail boom as seen on the museum example in the foreground. This proved to have been a design mistake as it created control problems for the pilot. Later-production units and rebuilt units had the tail rotor moved to the right-hand side of the tail boom. (*Paul and Loren Hannah*)

(**Opposite, above**) The lack of front fuselage landing lights and the chin turret armed with two weapons instead of a single weapon identify this preserved AH-1G Huey Cobra as a post-1966-built aircraft. The two-weapon chin turret was designated the TAT-141 and was armed with the XM28A1 armament sub-system consisting of either two M134 7.62mm mini-guns or a single mini-gun and a single M129 40mm grenade-launcher. (*Paul and Loren Hannah*)

(**Opposite, below**) Visible is an analogue instrument panel for the pilot on an AH-1G Huey Cobra. To offset heat build-up within the sealed canopy of the aircraft the builder had designed it with a forced draft air blower system. This proved completely inadequate in South-East Asia and led to the design and fitting of an air-conditioner system for the AH-1G referred to as the Environmental Control Unit (ECU). (*DOD*)

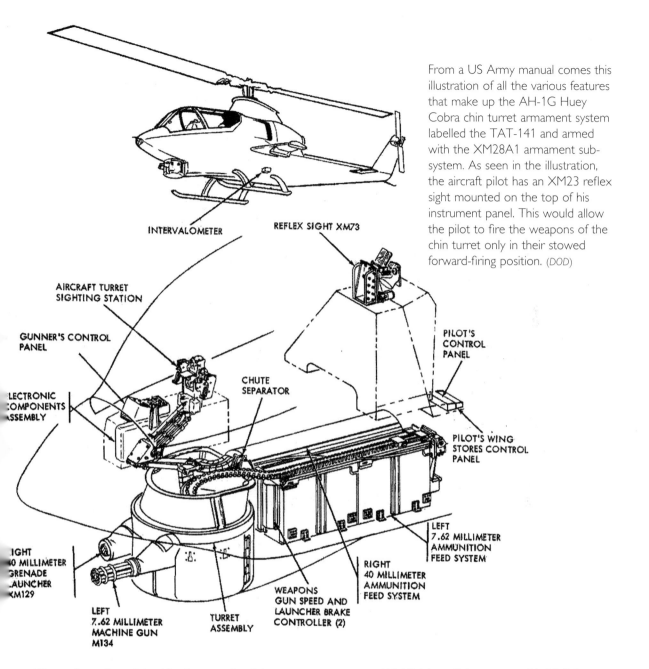

From a US Army manual comes this illustration of all the various features that make up the AH-1G Huey Cobra chin turret armament system labelled the TAT-141 and armed with the XM28A1 armament sub-system. As seen in the illustration, the aircraft pilot has an XM23 reflex sight mounted on the top of his instrument panel. This would allow the pilot to fire the weapons of the chin turret only in their stowed forward-firing position. (*DOD*)

INTERVALOMETER

REFLEX SIGHT XM73

AIRCRAFT TURRET
SIGHTING STATION

GUNNER'S CONTROL
PANEL

PILOT'S
CONTROL
PANEL

ELECTRONIC
COMPONENTS
ASSEMBLY

CHUTE
SEPARATOR

PILOT'S WING
STORES CONTROL
PANEL

LEFT
7.62 MILLIMETER
AMMUNITION
FEED SYSTEM

RIGHT
40 MILLIMETER
GRENADE
LAUNCHER
XM129

RIGHT
40 MILLIMETER
AMMUNITION
FEED SYSTEM

LEFT
7.62 MILLIMETER
MACHINE GUN
M134

TURRET
ASSEMBLY

WEAPONS
GUN SPEED AND
LAUNCHER BRAKE
CONTROLLER (2)

(**Opposite, above**) In this photograph of the gunner seat on an AH-1G Huey Cobra we see his XM28 turret sighting system. By moving it the gunner could slew the weapon-armed chin turret in various directions as well as upward or downward. As soon as the gunner removed his hand from the sighting system the chin turret would automatically revert to its forward-facing stowed position. (*Bell*)

(**Opposite, below**) Following the Vietnam War the US Army upgraded part of its inventory of AH-1G Huey Cobra units with the four-round M56 TOW anti-tank missile-launcher kit seen here. The early TOWs had an approximate range of 4,000 yards and were able to penetrate between 430mm and 630mm of steel armour. (*Chris Hughes*)

(**Above**) To aim and fire the eight available TOW anti-tank missiles when the AH-1G Huey Cobra was fitted with two of the M56 launcher units, the helicopter came with the M65 Telescopic Sight Unit (TSU), seen here with its protective flaps in the closed position in the fuselage nose of a museum AH-1G. The TSU was stabilized and had a wide-view two-power magnification and a thirteen-power narrow-view magnification. (*Chris Hughes*)

(**Opposite, above**) Those AH-1G Huey Cobra units upgraded with the four-round M56 TOW anti-tank missile armament kit and the M65 TSU were eventually redesignated the AH-1Q. With additional modifications they became the AH-1S model seen here. This is an upgraded early-production unit as it retains the rounded crew canopy of the AH-1G and AH-1Q models that preceded it. (*Paul and Loren Hannah*)

(**Opposite, below**) Pictured is an early-production AH-1S armed with rocket pods and the M56 TOW anti-tank missile armament kit. The 2.75in rocket pods were dubbed 'Hog pods' in South-East Asia. When a Huey Cobra was fitted with one rocket pod on either side of its fuselage it was referred to as a 'Hog' and when armed with two rocket pods on either side of the fuselage it became known as a 'Heavy Hog'. (*Paul and Loren Hannah*)

(**Opposite, above**) Belonging to a privately-run aviation museum and taking part in an air show is this rare trainer version of the AH1-P that was designated the TAH-1P. The AH-1P was the first model of the Huey Cobra to feature the new flat-panel cockpit canopy that became standard on later-production models of the helicopter. Like the original rounded canopy, it was not armoured. (*Paul and Loren Hannah*)

(**Opposite, below**) US Army soldiers are showing foreign military students the process of arming an AH-1 Huey Cobra with 2.75in rockets. The Mighty Mouse 2.75in rockets of the Vietnam War are long gone and were replaced post-conflict by the 70mm Hydra rockets. They are also sometimes referred to as Wrap-Around Fin Aerial Rockets (WAFARs) and come in various versions. (*DOD*)

(**Above**) The last version of the AH-1 Huey Cobra series was the AH-1F model pictured here. The flat-plate canopy appeared on new-built AH-1S units beginning in 1977. The three-barrel 20mm M197 cannon in the chin turret appeared with the AH-1E model starting in 1988 and on all subsequent models. An external spotting feature of the AH-1F is the air data sensor mounted on the upper right side of the canopy. (*DOD*)

(**Above**) The sad fate of the AH-1F Huey Cobra pictured here is to act as a non-operational training aid in an aircraft recovery drill. The air data sensor support arm has been pressed up against the canopy. Another external spotting feature of the 'F' model Huey Cobra was the large olive-drab blister at the front of the rotor transmission unit for a laser tracking system that was never fitted. (*DOD*)

(**Opposite, above**) With the combat effectiveness of the US Army AH-1G Huey Cobra proved in South-East Asia, the USMC decided that a larger two-engine version with a more powerful armament mixture was desired. This would result in the fielding of the AH-1J named the 'Sea Cobra' seen here. This example is armed only with a three-barrel 20mm M197 cannon in its chin turret. (*DOD*)

(**Opposite, below**) On display at a museum is this preserved AH-1J Sea Cobra. The USMC ordered forty-nine units of the 'J' model Sea Cobra in 1968. The first production example came off the assembly line in the following year. Testing of the initial production examples of the AH-J Sea Cobra took place between 1970 and early 1971. The first operational unit equipped with the aircraft was formed in the summer of 1971. (*Chris Hughes*)

(**Above**) The added power of the second engine on the AH-1J Sea Cobra allowed the USMC to consider equipping it with a much wider range of weapons than was possible with the US Army single engine-powered AH-1G Huey Cobra. One of the weapons tested by the USMC on the AH-1J Sea Cobra is the air-to-air AIM-9L Sidewinder missile seen here attached to one of the aircraft's two stub wings. (*DOD*)

(**Opposite, above**) Along with the US Army the USMC saw the need to provide its attack helicopter inventory with the ability to fire the TOW anti-tank missile. This led to the development of the AH-1T version sometimes referred to as the 'Improved Sea Cobra'. It in turn was replaced by the AH-1W Super Cobra seen here, which is also referred to as the 'Whiskey Cobra'. (*DOD*)

(**Opposite, below**) Mechanics are shown working on the chin turret mechanism of an AH-1W Super Cobra. Clearly visible in this picture is the weapon sighting unit in the fuselage nose. It is a far more advanced version of the M65 Telescopic Sight Unit (TSU) fitted to the US Army AH-1Q in 1975, which was a daylight-only system. That fitted to the Super Cobra contains both a thermal-imaging sight as well as a Forward-Looking Infrared (FLIR) radar system. (*DOD*)

(**Above**) The AH-1W Super Cobra seen here is 58ft in length and has a height of 13ft 9in. The stub wings on either side of the aircraft fuselage give it a width of 10ft 9in. Empty it weighs 10,200lb and has a maximum take-off weight of 14,750lb. Its two engines provide it with a top speed of 218mph and a range of 365 miles. The helicopter service ceiling is 12,200ft. (*DOD*)

(**Opposite, above**) Marine Corps personnel are shown checking on the four-round M272 launcher unit attached to the right-hand stub wing of an AH-1W Super Cobra, armed with four AGM-114 Hellfire missiles. During Operation DESERT STORM in 1991 the AH-1W accounted for 97 Iraqi tanks and 104 Iraqi armoured personnel carriers. Besides the 70mm Hydra rocket, the M272 can be armed with 127mm (5in) Zuni rockets. (*DOD*)

(**Opposite, below**) Recognizing the threat from infrared-guided anti-aircraft missiles, the AH-1W Super Cobra features a number of protection devices. Visible just behind the rotor mast of the helicopter pictured here is the red-tinted AN/ALQ-144 Countermeasure Set. It is an omni-directional, active, continuous-operation system that confuses and decoys incoming infrared missiles away from the helicopter. (*DOD*)

Despite the continued interest from the USMC in acquiring the AH-64 Apache, funding constraints made that impossible. The back-up plan was the rebuilding of the AH-1W Super Cobra fleet into the AH-1Z version named the 'Viper' seen here. An external spotting feature of the 'Z' model is the new ball-shaped AN/AAQ-30 Hawkeye Target Sight System (TSS) at the fuselage nose. (*DOD*)

In this picture of an AH-1Z Viper, the AN/AAQ-30 Hawkeye TSS is seen in its stowed position. Other external spotting features of the AH-1Z Viper pictured are the new composite four-bladed rotor as well as all the fuselage fairings not seen on its predecessor. Like the AH-1W, the AH-1Z can be armed with air-to-air missiles as well as anti-radar missiles that home in on anti-aircraft guidance radar units. (*DOD*)

The pilots and the gunner/co-pilot on the AH-1Z Viper are shown wearing the helmet-mounted sight and display system referred to as 'Top Owl'. The head-up display within the helmet allows the pilots to fly their aircraft and fight an enemy without looking away, day or night. All the information they need is superimposed on their visors, which they can see through. *(DOD)*

With an empty weight of 12,300lb the AH-1Z Viper has a maximum weight of 18,500lb. Its top speed is 255mph with a cruising speed of 184mph. Range is 426 miles, which decreases according to the weight of weapon loads. The aircraft has a service ceiling of 20,000ft. For storage on US Navy ships the helicopter rotor blades have an automatic folding feature. *(DOD)*

Besides the AN/ALQ-144 Countermeasure Set seen just behind the rotor mast on this AH-1Z Viper there is another infrared guided missile countermeasure device. It is mounted on the top of the aircraft's stub wing and is designated the ALE-47 chaff/flare dispenser. Pilots can set the device to operate in one of three different modes: manual, semi-automatic or fully automatic. (DOD)

On board a US Navy warship a mechanic is shown screwing in a new barrel to the M197 20mm cannon on the chin turret of an AH-1Z Viper. The helicopter has storage space for 750 rounds of 20mm ammunition. The stub wings on the Viper are wider than those on the previous AH-1W Super Cobra, allowing for more weapons to be mounted. (DOD)

The search for the replacement for the cancelled AH-56A Cheyenne began in the early 1970s under the programme name Advance Attack Helicopter (AAH). A number of companies submitted prototypes for the US Army's evaluation. Pictured is the Bell contender labelled the M409. In a reverse of the Cheyenne and the AH-1 Huey Cobra, Bell put the pilot in the front of the fuselage with the gunner/co-pilot in a raised seat behind him. *(Bell)*

In this picture we see a non-operational mock-up of the Hughes contender for the US Army AAH programme. The firm designated it the Model 77. Instead of the XM188 30mm cannon that the other competitors planned for their versions of the AAH, Hughes proposed arming the Model 77 with a 30mm cannon of their own design designated the M230 Chain Gun. *(Hughes)*

(**Above**) Pictured is the Hughes-designed and built AH-64A Apache. It can be identified as such by the tapered end of the fuselage cheek fairing on the right-hand side of the aircraft. There was a near-identical fairing on the opposite side of the helicopter's fuselage. The first flight of a prototype Apache designated the YAH-64 took place on 30 September 1975. (*Paul and Loren Hannah*)

(**Opposite, above**) In this picture of an AH-64A Apache during Operation DESERT STORM in 1991 we can see the shape of the cheek fairing on the left-hand side of the aircraft. It was a near-copy of that on the other side of the helicopter's fuselage. Because the pilots of the Apache enter and exit the aircraft from the right-hand side only, there was no step-cutout on the left-hand-side cheek fairing. (*DOD*)

(**Opposite, below**) Preparing for a take-off in Iraq following Operation IRAQI FREEDOM in 2003 is an AH-64D Apache. It can be identified as such by the cheek fairing design seen on the right-hand side of the helicopter. Rather than being tapered at the front of the fuselage as it was on the AH-64A, the fairing now curved around to the very front of the aircraft's fuselage. (*DOD*)

(**Opposite, above**) The AH-64D Apache pictured here contained a great deal more avionics than the original AH-64A model. To accommodate some of these new electronic devices the shape of the cheek fairing on the left-hand side ran to the front of the fuselage and had a pronounced rear upward sweep that is visible in this picture. Production of the AH-64D was authorized in 1995. (*DOD*)

(**Opposite, below**) In this picture of an AH-64D Apache undergoing maintenance some of the avionics located in the left-hand-side fuselage cheek fairing are visible. The US Army had asked Congress in 1991 following Operation DESERT STORM for funding to purchase an upgraded model of the Apache to be designated the AH-64B. However, that programme was cancelled in 1992 and a proposed 'C' model also went nowhere. (*DOD*)

(**Above**) When the AH-64D Apache is fitted with the removable mast-mounted Fire Control Radar (FCR) named the 'Longbow', seen on the helicopter in the foreground, it becomes the Longbow Apache (LBA). It automatically identifies those targets that pose the most serious threat to the helicopter so the flight crew can quickly take appropriate action. (*DOD*)

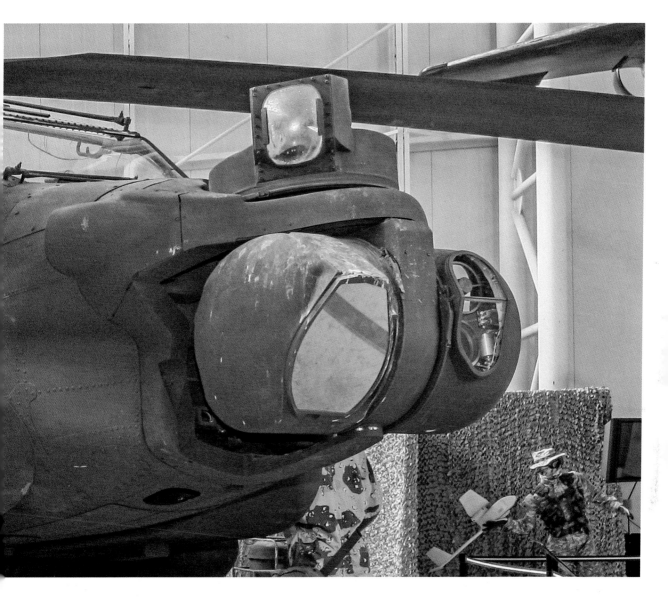

(**Opposite, above**) Soldiers load an AH-64 Apache series helicopter with AGM-114 series Hellfire missiles, which entered American military service in 1982. The Hellfire has come in a number of progressively-improved versions with some optimized for specific roles. There are those intended for the destruction of heavily-armoured tanks, with others designed for soft targets such as buildings and unarmoured vehicles. (*DOD*)

(**Opposite, below**) In its original configuration the AGM-114 Hellfire missile pictured could be employed in two different modes. The first was autonomous in which the Apache that fired the missile also painted the target with the laser energy for it to home in on. The second type of firing mode was referred to as remote and involved a laser designation aimed at the target from another source. (*DOD*)

(**Above**) In this picture taken at a US Army museum can be seen the original Target and Designation Sight/Pilot Night Vision Sensor (TADS/PNVS) on an AH-64A Apache. The TADS comprises the bottom portion of the device with a thermal camera and a daylight TV camera with a 127-power magnification. The PNVS that allows the pilot to fly in darkness is the uppermost portion of the device. (*Paul and Loren Hannah*)

Pictured is the latest version of the Apache introduced into service in 2012 and designated the AH-64E Guardian. It is fitted with the Modernized Target and Designation Sight/Pilot Night Vision Sensor (M-TADS/PNVS) that was fielded on the AH-64D in 2005. The only external difference between it and the original version is in the configuration of the PNVS component located above the TADS component. *(DOD)*

Control of both the original Target and Designation Sight/Pilot Night Vision Sensor (TADS/PNVS) and the modernized version labelled the M-TADS/PNVS is done with helmet-mounted sights, an example of which is seen here on the pilot of an Apache. The official designation of the headgear for the flight crews of the Apache series is the Integrated Helmet and Display Sighting System (IHADSS). *(DOD)*

To hone the skills of the pilots and gunner/co-pilots on the AH-64 Apache series and at the same time minimize the flight hours on the helicopters themselves, simulators are a very cost-effective method. The multi-function instrument panel on the simulator pictured here recreates the gunner/co-pilot's position on either a 'D' or 'E' model Apache. With a simulator there is no limit on the amount of weaponry that can be expended. (*DOD*)

A soldier loads a Hydra 70 rocket into a pod on an AH-64 Apache series helicopter. The name Hydra refers to the nine-headed serpent of Greek mythology and symbolizes the multiple warhead configurations available for the rocket, including a high-explosive (HE) version and a specialized anti-personnel version. The 70 indicates the number of millimeters when converted from 2.75in. (*DOD*)

On a firing range an AH-64A Apache unleashes some of its Hydra 70 rockets at a target. The 70mm Hydra rockets have a maximum range of 11,500 yards and an effective range of less than 5,000 yards. All the various models of the Apache series have four weapon pylons, two on either side of the aircraft attached to the stub wings. (*DOD*)

For short-range engagements the AH-64 Apache series helicopter still depends on the M230 Chain Gun seen here. The 120lb weapon is extremely compact with a length of only 64.5in, a width of 10in and a height of 11.8in. Unlike the Hydra 70 rockets that remain area-fire weapons, the Chain Gun is suitable for pinpoint targets. (*DOD*)

On a target range an AH-64A Apache is shown firing its below-fuselage M230 30mm Chain Gun. The weapon is slewed as well as elevated and depressed hydraulically. The gun is fired electrically. In theory the maximum rate of fire is between 600 and 650 rounds per minute. In reality, the maximum rate of fire is approximately 300 rounds per minute and thereafter requires a ten-minute cooling-off period. (*DOD*)

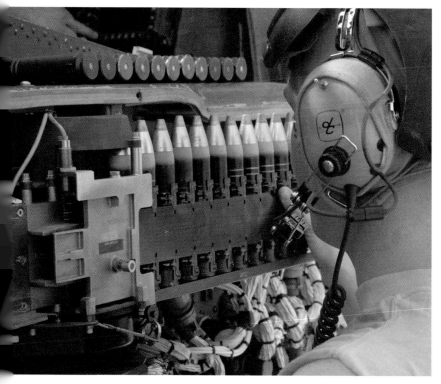

A soldier is shown loading 30mm rounds into the magazine of an AH-64 series Apache. The aircraft can carry up to 1,200 rounds of 30mm ammunition. The weapon fires two types of rounds: the M789 High-Explosive Dual-Purpose (HEDP) and the M799 High-Explosive Incendiary (HEI). Both rounds are very effective against exposed personnel and unarmoured vehicles. (*DOD*)

(**Opposite, above**) The oversized cheek fairings on either side of this AH-63E Apache Guardian fuselage are now referred to as the Enhanced Forward Avionics Bays (EFABs). This particular helicopter has an adapter on the top of the rotor hub for mounting the mast-mounted Longbow FCR. Note the snow shoes attached to the three-wheel landing gear of the helicopter. (*DOD*)

(**Opposite, below**) Taking part in a training exercise is an AH-64D Apache. It has a length of 49ft 5in and a height of 12ft 7in. Empty it weighs 11,388lb and has a maximum take-off weight of 23,000lb. Its two engines coupled together give it a top speed of 227mph with a cruising speed of 182mph. Operational range is approximately 300 miles on external fuel tanks. (*DOD*)

(**Above**) An AH-64 series Apache, with its four rotor blades folded rearward, is shown here being loaded into a USAF C-5A Galaxy transport. The first combat action for the attack helicopter took place during Operation JUST CAUSE, the American military invasion of Panama in 1989. There were a number of teething problems that were uncovered in the brief conflict that led to some quick design fixes. (*DOD*)

Visible are both an AH-64D Longbow Apache (LBA) distinguished by the radar pod atop the mast and two standard AH-64D Apaches. Such was the US Army's faith in the Apache that it was selected to lead the opening attack on the Iraqi air defence system during the American military invasion of Iraq in 1991, which was referred to as Operation DESERT STORM. A total of 227 units of the Apache would eventually take part in the 100-hour conflict. *(DOD)*

An AH-64E Guardian is shown during a training activity. The mast-mounted Longbow FCR weighs approximately 250lb and can scan 360 degrees when looking for aerial threats. When employed scanning for ground threats it can scan in a 270-degree arc and identify over 200 potential targets at the same time and display that information to the pilots on multi-function digital screens. *(DOD)*

Chapter Four

Special-Purpose Helicopters

From the beginning of its long career with the American armed forces, the helicopter has displayed a remarkable versatility and ability to perform a wide variety of different roles. With that being said, some have been optimized to conduct one major role, such as attack helicopters. There have been other dedicated helicopters acquired for specific missions. However, as time went on some of these helicopters were modified to serve new roles.

Seasprite

In 1956, the US Navy issued a requirement for a new multi-purpose helicopter that was primarily intended to operate from aircraft carriers in the CSAR/SAR role. Kaman won the competition in 1957 with a single-engine helicopter they referred to as the K-20. It entered US Navy service in 1962 as the HU2K-1 Seasprite, later becoming the UH-2A in 1962. The engine on the helicopter produced 1,250hp.

A total of 88 units of the UH-2A along with 102 units of a slightly different version labelled the UH-2B were built. Considered underpowered, most were rebuilt with two engines coupled together, each engine producing 1,250hp. In this configuration the Seasprite was designated the UH-2C.

Two sub-variants of the UH-2C were the HH-2C, of which six were fielded, and sixty-seven units of the HH-2D. Both were optimized for the CSAR role. The HH-2C was armed with three machine guns. The more numerous HH-2D was not armed.

Anti-Submarine Seasprite

Twenty units of the HH-2Ds were eventually converted into a heavily-armed model labelled the SH-2D. The prefix letter 'S' stands for anti-submarine. The SH-2D was fitted with the original version of the Light Airborne Multi-Purpose System (LAMPS). The system works by tying together all the sensors of both helicopters and warships in near real-time to identify and destroy any threats to a US Navy battlegroup, be they underwater or on the surface.

The SH-2D was followed by the SH-2F, which began entering US Navy service in 1973. Like the earlier SH-2D it was fitted with LAMPS. Forty-nine units of the SH-2F were new-built aircraft, with the remaining units being rebuilt examples of the earlier models of the helicopter. The 'F' model Seasprite lasted in US Navy service until 1994.

Seasprite Rescue

Only a single US Navy helicopter pilot received the Medal of Honor during the Vietnam War. He was awarded his country's highest honour for his action flying a UH-2A Seasprite during a daring rescue attempt. The official citation detailing his actions is as follows:

'For conspicuous gallantry and intrepidity at the risk of his life above and beyond the call of duty on 19 June 1968 as pilot and aircraft commander of a search and rescue helicopter, attached to Helicopter Support Squadron 7 during operations against enemy forces in North Vietnam.

Launched shortly after midnight to attempt the rescue of two downed aviators, Lieutenant (then Lieutenant, Junior Grade) Lassen skillfully piloted his aircraft over unknown and hostile terrain to a steep, tree-covered hill on which the survivors had been located. Although enemy fire was being directed at the helicopter, he initially landed in a clear area near the base of the hill, but, due to the dense undergrowth, the survivors could not reach the helicopter.

With the aid of flare illumination, Lieutenant Lassen successfully accomplished a hover between two trees at the survivors' position. Illumination was abruptly lost as the last of the flares were expended, and the helicopter collided with a tree, commencing a sharp descent. Expertly righting his aircraft and maneuvering clear, Lieutenant Lassen remained in the area, determined to make another rescue attempt, and encouraged the downed aviators while awaiting resumption of flare illumination.

After another unsuccessful, illuminated, rescue attempt, and with his fuel dangerously low and his aircraft significantly damaged, he launched again and commenced another approach in the face of the continuing enemy opposition. When flare illumination was again lost, Lieutenant Lassen, fully aware of the dangers in clearly revealing his position to the enemy, turned on his landing lights and completed the landing. On this attempt, the survivors were able to make their way to the helicopter.

En route to the coast, he encountered and successfully evaded additional hostile anti-aircraft fire and, with fuel for only minutes of flight remaining, landed safely aboard USS *Jouett* (DLG-29). Lt. Lassen's extraordinary heroism at the risk of his own life, above and beyond the call of duty, are in keeping with the highest traditions of the military service and reflect great credit upon himself, his unit, and the US Navy.'

The last model of the Seasprite in service with the US Navy was the SH-2G, which was nicknamed the 'Super Seasprite'. The SH-2G inventory consisted of eighteen rebuilt units of the SH-2F and six new-built units. They were in service with the US Navy from 1991 until 2001.

Sea King

Another helicopter that became operational with the US Navy in the early 1960s was the twin-engine Sikorsky SH-3A, officially nicknamed the 'Sea King'. The two engines coupled together each produced 1,400hp. The primary role of the SH-3A was ASW.

The biggest threat to the US Navy surface fleet during the Cold War (1949–91) was the large number of Soviet navy submarines, both conventionally-powered and nuclear-powered. A total of 245 units of the SH-3A were built for the US Navy.

As time went on and technology improved, more advanced versions of the Sea King for the ASW role appeared with LAMPS fitted. These included 75 units of the SH-3D and 167 units of the SH-3H. The majority of these were rebuilt SH-3A units. Besides the ASW role, other Sea Kings were converted into dedicated models for the CSAR/SAR, utility and minesweeper roles, each with its own designation. The last units of the helicopter were retired from US Navy service in 2006.

Seahawk

The replacement for the US Navy Seasprite in the ASW role was the Sikorsky SH-60B, which was officially nicknamed the 'Seahawk'. The first of 181 units entered service in 1984. It was based on a modified version of the US Army's UH-60A Black Hawk and intended to operate from the entire range of US Navy surface ships, not just aircraft carriers. Like the later models of the Seasprite, the SH-60B was fitted with LAMPS.

A version of the Seahawk intended to replace the SH-3 Sea King series for ASW operations from aircraft carriers received the designation SH-60F. The first of seventy-six units entered service in 1989 and received the unofficial nickname 'Ocean Hawk'. Like the SH-60B, the 'F' model Seahawk was fitted with LAMPS.

A stripped-down variant of the SH-60F was the HH-60H deployed by the US Navy from aircraft carriers. Its primary role was CSAR/SAR and it therefore received the unofficial nickname 'Rescue Hawk'. The US Navy took forty-two units into service. These and all the remaining SH-60B, SH-60F and HH-60H Seahawks were retired from US Navy service in 2015 with the advent of newer models.

Next-Generation Seahawks

In an effort to standardize its Seahawk inventory, in 2008 the US Navy took into service the first of 291 units of the MH-60R version of the Seahawk. This was the replacement for the SH-60B and SH-60F in the ASW role but far more capable, able to deal equally well with undersea and surface threats with the latest in avionics and weaponry.

From a US Navy online article dated 23 January 2006 is this passage explaining what the 'R' model of the Seahawk brings to the US Navy:

Unlike the SH-60B and SH-60F which it will replace, the MH-60R features electronic support measures, airborne low-frequency sonar, a multi-mission radar upgrade (including ISAR), forward-looking infrared (FLIR), and a weapons suite including torpedoes and Hellfire missiles ... It is designed to operate from frigates, destroyers, cruisers and aircraft carriers alike.

A less complex and therefore more affordable version of the Seahawk is designated the MH-60S, of which the US Navy has taken into service 237 units starting in 2002. It is based on the US Army UH-60L Black Hawk and is the US Navy's replacement for the CH-46 Sea Knight, which was retired in 2004. Its unofficial nickname is 'Knighthawk' and depending on its mission kit, it can perform any number of roles as explained in the *US Navy Program Guide 2015*: 'The MH-60S provides surface and mine countermeasure warfare capabilities, as well as robust Naval Special Warfare, search and rescue, combat search and rescue, and logistics capability, with air-to-ground weapons and the same FLIR and Link16 capability as the MH-60R.'

The logistic capability of the MH-60S mentioned in the extract above is officially labelled by the US Navy as vertical replenishment (VERTREP). This was a manner of ship-to-ship replenishment pioneered by the US Navy in the early 1960s in which helicopters pick up and deliver pre-loaded pallets. Despite the biggest advantage – that ships no longer have to be directly connected to each other to receive supplies – it remains a somewhat dangerous process for all involved and is often limited by weather and strong winds.

Unmanned Helicopters

Between 1960 and 1969, the US Navy took into service 732 units of a small unmanned aerial vehicle (UAV) designated the Drone Anti-Submarine Helicopter (DASH) in several versions. DASH was intended to operate from flight decks of smaller US Navy warships such as frigates and destroyer escorts.

Armament on the DASH consisted of two torpedoes or a single nuclear depth-charge. The programme was not a success, with approximately 400 DASH units lost in accidents, resulting in the programme's cancellation in 1971. The US Navy's replacement for the DASH was the SH-2F Seasprite.

In 2009, the US Navy took into service the first of thirty units of the Northrop Grumman MQ-8B UAV that was officially nicknamed the 'Fire Scout'. It was designed to be operated from a number of different types of warships. It is based on a much-modified two-man civilian helicopter known as the Sikorsky S-333.

The MQ-8B has been fitted with an entire range of electronic sensors, allowing it to provide reconnaissance and precision targeting information. It has also been successfully tested with a number of weapon kits. The MQ-8B is being supplement by a larger version based on the Bell 407 commercial helicopter, which is designated the MQ-8C Fire Scout.

As early as 2012 the US Army began looking into a UAV helicopter programme of its own. In response Lockheed Martin, in conjunction with Kaman, built prototypes of an aircraft labelled the 'K-Max'. It was envisioned only as an aerial logistical platform. The prototypes were tested in Afghanistan. As of 2016, the US Army had not committed to its acquisition.

Sea Dragon

The US Navy acquired fifteen units of a modified version of the USMC CH-53A Sea Stallion, labelled the RH-53A. It was intended for the Airborne Mine Counter-measures (AMCM) mission. When the USMC took into service the upgraded 'D' model of the Sea Stallion, the US Navy took on thirty units for the AMCM mission and designated it the RH-53D. Neither of these helicopters remains in US Navy service.

The US Navy decided that the RH-53D was not powerful enough nor had sufficient fuel capacity to perform the AMCM mission. This resulted in the delivery of a modified CH-53E Super Stallion helicopter designated the MH-53E and officially nicknamed the 'Sea Dragon'. It disposes of mines by mechanical, magnetic and acoustic means. Besides the AMCM role, the Sea Dragon performs VERTREP. The US Navy expects to keep the MH-53E in service until 2025.

Huskie

The USAF began taking delivery of the first of eighteen units of the Kaman K-600 in 1958. It was designated the H-43A and officially nicknamed the 'Huskie'. The single piston engine on the H-43A was replaced on a subsequent model with an 825hp gas turbine engine, resulting in the designation change to H-43B. The USAF placed an order for 200 units of the H-43B in the late 1950s, which was redesignated the HH-43B in 1962.

Those HH-43B Huskies employed by the USAF during the Vietnam War were primarily employed as flying firetrucks at air bases in South Vietnam. A specialized CSAR model of the Huskie employed during the Vietnam War by the USAF was also powered by a single gas turbine engine and labelled the HH-43F. Six were lost during the conflict.

Taken from a 1992 USAF historical publication titled *Search and Rescue in South-East Asia*, author Earl H. Tilford describes what came with the HH-43F Huskie:

> The HH-43F represented a significant improvement over the B models and provided the Air Rescue Service with a limited combat aircrew recovery capability … To protect the aircrews and passengers, the new model carried 800lbs of titanium armor distributed in 0.5-inch sheets around the crew compartment and over the engine cowling. The F model engine … produced 1,150hp, 400hp more than the engine in the standard Huskie.

Jolly Green Giant

Impressed with the US Navy's SH-3A Sea King, the USAF ordered a larger more capable version that the company referred to as the S-61R. In USAF service it became the CH-3C, which was followed by a version with more powerful engines labelled the CH-3E. The latter in turn was replaced by another upgraded model

Jolly Green Giant Medal of Honor Winner

As their pilots constantly placed themselves in harm's way on every rescue mission attempted, it is not surprising that a USAF Search and Rescue (SAR) pilot named Gerald O. Young would be awarded his nation's highest honour in 1968 by President Lyndon B. Johnson. The action that resulted in his Medal of Honor award appears in this description from an online USAF history site:

'Shortly before midnight on Nov. 8, 1967, Captain Young, the commander of an HH-3E rescue helicopter, was dispatched to evacuate the survivors of a U.S. Army reconnaissance team. The soldiers were surrounded and about to be captured in enemy-held territory in the Laotian Panhandle. Two helicopters had already been lost trying to rescue them.

Captain Young and his crew were flying as back-up for another helicopter on this night operation. The first aircraft managed to pick up three members of the team before extensive battle damage forced it to withdraw. The commander of the craft advised Captain Young that intense enemy fire made the rescue of two soldiers left behind all but impossible. Accompanying gunships were also running low on fuel and ammunition.

Intent on completing the evacuation Captain Young guided his helicopter down into the flare-lit darkness, touching down on a slope not far from the two soldiers. Both wounded, they were loaded aboard under heavy attack with enemy troops closing in. As it moved forward for take-off, the helicopter was fired on at point-blank range. It plunged downward and crashed in flames in an upside-down position. Captain Young dropped out of a cockpit window and rolled down the slope, his parachute afire. Although badly burned, he beat out the flames and gave aid to another crew member, a sergeant, who had also escaped. He then tried to reach the burning helicopter but was driven back by the intense heat. When enemy troops approached the crash scene, he led them away from the wounded sergeant hidden in the underbrush.

At dawn, Captain Young reached a clearing and helped to pinpoint his position for searching aircraft with flares and radio signals, but he broke contact when he realized that he was being used as bait by enemy gunners in the area. He again concealed himself in the dense foliage and continued to evade throughout the day despite the mounting pain of his burns. After 17 hours, Captain Young was finally rescued by a helicopter that he attracted with his radio and by firing tracers with his revolver. He then immediately informed his rescuers of the position of his fellow crew member.'

referred to as the HH-3E, which consisted of eight new-built units and fifty rebuilt CH-3E units.

It was the HH-3E version that was sent to South-East Asia in 1965 by the USAF to perform the CSAR role. It was here that it was unofficially nicknamed the 'Jolly Green Giant' (after a make-believe television marketing campaign figure) based on their two-tone drab green and tan camouflage paint schemes.

The HH-3E was powered by two 1,250hp engines coupled together, which provided it with a top speed of 160mph at 7,000ft and a maximum operational ceiling of 12,000ft. It could cruise at 100mph at 10,000ft, out of range of enemy 23mm and 37mm anti-aircraft guns.

With externally-added fuel tanks the HH-3E had an operational range of 500 miles. Eventually it was fitted with an in-flight refuelling probe that gave it almost unlimited range. Unlike its predecessors, the HH-3E was both armoured and armed to increase its survivability in combat.

The HH-3E was also fitted with a hydraulic rescue hoist on the right-hand side of the fuselage over the crew door. It was 250ft long and could lift up to 600lb. A total of twenty-one units were lost during the Vietnam War. By 1995, the last of the HH-3E units had been retired from USAF service.

Super Jolly Green Giant

The HH-3E Jolly Green Giants had a number of limitations that often compromised assigned missions. These included the helicopter's slow speed and insufficient defensive firepower. Another problem was the HH-3E's limited ability to hover at higher altitudes due to lack of sufficient engine power. It was at about this time that the USMC began deploying the twin-engine CH-53 series Sea Stallions to South Vietnam. The USAF believed it could be the helicopter they needed for the CSAR role.

In response, Sikorsky developed a modified CSAR version of the CH-53 series which the USAF labelled the HH-53B. Eight units arrived in South Vietnam in 1967. An upgraded model designated the HH-53C began arriving in South Vietnam the following year. Fifty-eight 'C' model units were eventually acquired by the USAF.

The HH-53B and HH-53C helicopters in South-East Asia soon picked up a couple of unofficial nicknames. One was the 'Super Jolly Green Giant', reflecting its massive size compared to the HH-3E Jolly Green Giant, and the other was the 'BUFF'. The latter was short for 'Big Ugly Fat F*cker', with the more polite version of that being the 'Big Ugly Fat Fellow'.

A description of what the HH-53 series brought to the USAF rescue units in South Vietnam appears in this passage from a 1992 USAF historical publication titled *Search and Rescue in South-East Asia* by Earl H. Tilford:

The Super Jolly Greens had all the avionics of the HH-3Es. Their biggest improvements were in lift power and defensive armament. Two GE-T64-3 turboshaft engines produced 3,080hp to increase lift power. On one occasion an HH-53B lifted an A-1E [fixed-wing single-engine aircraft] weighing 12,000 pounds and carried it 56 miles … This added lift power increased its hover capability by 40 percent to make crew recoveries from the higher mountain regions less hazardous.

Covert Mission Helicopters

The bulk of the USAF CH-3C helicopters deployed to South-East Asia in 1967 belonged to two units: the 20th and 21st Helicopter Squadrons. The former was nicknamed the 'Pony Express' and the latter the 'Dust Devils'. Despite their mundane unit designations and colourful nicknames, these units were in reality USAF Special Operations Force (SOF) units. They were tasked with running covert missions, typically involving the delivery into and recovery of unconventional warfare teams in the countries surrounding South Vietnam.

Besides its CH-3C helicopters, the 20th Helicopter Squadron also began using thirty-one units of the UH-1F Huey, some of which were later reconfigured as UH-1P gunships. Their job was to escort the CH-3C helicopters during their missions. Eventually they took into service the twin-engine UH-1N Huey, some of which were also converted into gunships. Reflecting their multi-coloured camouflage paint schemes, the Hueys were unofficially nicknamed the 'Green Hornets'.

In 1969, the Dust Devils took over the CH-3Cs and Hueys of the Pony Express as well as their missions. In 1970, the number of covert missions was greatly reduced as a new American president was trying to bring the war in South-East Asia to a close and reduce the number of American casualties. All the men and the helicopters of the Dust Devils stood down in 1972, with American military involvement in the war coming to an end in the following year.

The HH-53 series was faster than its predecessor and could reach a maximum altitude of 16,000ft. The former could hover at up to 6,500ft and the latter only 4,000ft. The operational range of both helicopters was unlimited with in-flight refuelling. Armament on the HH-3E was up to two 7.62mm machine guns with that on the HH-53 series consisting of a single-barrel 7.62mm machine gun and two mini-guns.

Despite being better armoured and armed than its predecessor, the HH-53 series was also a bigger target and twenty were lost during the Vietnam War as enemy air defence systems dramatically improved with radar guidance beginning in 1970. One of the HH-53 series helicopters was shot down over North Vietnam by an enemy fighter with an air-to-air missile.

Pave Low

In the 1980s the USAF as an experiment had eight of their remaining Vietnam War-vintage HH-53 series helicopters rebuilt from the ground up and fitted with the latest in avionics. They therefore became the MH-53H Pave Low. The word 'Pave' is an acronym for Precision Avionics Vectoring Equipment and the word 'Low' reflects the fact that the helicopter could now fly nap-of-the earth (NOE) around the clock and in adverse weather conditions.

The advanced capabilities of the MH-53H Pave Low soon caught the attention of the Air Force Special Operations Command (AFSOC). This resulted in the former CSAR helicopter assuming new roles such as long-range infiltration and exfiltration. Positive results with the MH-53H Pave Low led to an upgraded model designated the MH-53J Pave Low III.

One of the most important later additions to the MH-53J Pave Low III was referred to as the Interactive Defensive Avionics System/Multi-Mission Advanced Tactical Terminal, or IDAS/MATT. A description of the device appeared in an online USAF article dated 19 October 1998:

> A color, multifunctional, night-vision compatible digital map screen is the most visible hardware in the system. Located on the helicopter's instrument panel, the display gives an MH-53 crew a clearer picture of the battlefield. Crews have access to near real-time events, including the aircrew's flight route, man-made hazards such as power lines and even enemy electronic threats that are 'over-the-horizon'. Transmissions are beamed from a satellite to the helicopter's computer and then decoded. The data from the screen provides a perspective of potential threats and their lethal threat radius.

Reflecting the heightened level of capabilities provided by IDAS/MATT, the MH-53J Pave Low III was relabelled as MH-53M Pave Low IV. Despite this enhancement, all the Pave Low helicopters were retired from USAF service in 2008. The 2009 replacement for the MH-53M was the CV-22B Osprey. Like its predecessor, it is equipped with an integrated threat countermeasure system, terrain-following radar, forward-looking infrared sensor and other advanced avionics systems.

Pave Hawk

In 1981, the USAF chose a modified version of the US Army's UH-60A Black Hawk as the replacement for the HH-3E Jolly Green Giant in both the CSAR and SAR roles. The helicopter was designated the HH-60G by the USAF and originally assigned the name 'Credible Hawk', which was later changed to 'Pave Hawk'. Operational status with the Pave Hawk was achieved in 1987.

A much more advanced variant of the HH-60G Pave Hawk for the AFSOF was assigned the designation MH-60G Pave Hawk. With the disbandment of the only AFSOF unit equipped with the MH-60G Pave Hawk in the early 1990s, its sixteen helicopters were reassigned to the CSAR and SAR roles and were redesignated as HH-60G Pave Hawks.

Beginning in 1999, the USAF began looking for an upgraded Pave Hawk. In 2104, funding was authorized for the USAF to order 112 units of a more capable version of the HH-60G Pave Hawk. That new and yet unbuilt helicopter has been labelled the

HH-60W Pave Hawk, with the initial production units to be delivered by 2020 and the last by 2029.

Tarhe

In its quest to find a suitable gas turbine engine-powered heavy-lift helicopter to replace the piston-engine-powered CH-47 Mojave, in the early 1960s the US Army settled on ordering a Sikorsky-designed-and-built twin-engine helicopter they designated the CH-54A and officially nicknamed the 'Tarhe'. Its unofficial nicknames became 'Skyhook' and the 'Flying Crane'. Both nicknames referred to a cargo hook under its fuselage for carrying a wide variety of under-slung loads.

In total the US Army ordered ninety-one units of the Tarhe, divided between fifty-four of the original 'A' model and thirty-seven upgraded 'B' model units. During the Vietnam War, the primary role of the CH-54 series was to lift large and heavy items of equipment, such as artillery pieces, to otherwise inaccessible locations. It also recovered downed aircraft. Of those deployed to South-East Asia, nine were lost. The remaining Tarhes would remain in US Army service until 1991 when its job was taken over by the CH-47 Chinook series.

Cayuse

In 1959, the US Army began a search for a replacement of its Korean War-vintage piston-engine-powered OH-13 Sioux and OH-23 Raven series observation helicopters. The replacement would have to be gas turbine engine-powered. Thirteen companies submitted design proposals, with three eventually asked to provide prototypes for the Light Observation Helicopter (LOH) competition.

Eventually the army decided that both Hiller and Hughes LOH designs met the requirements, with the winner to be determined by price. Hughes Aircraft offered the lowest price for a total of 714 helicopters in 1965. The new LOH was designated the OH-6A and assigned the official nickname 'Cayuse'. It had a crew of two: a pilot and an observer. The first production example came off the assembly line in 1966.

In 1967, the Cayuse was rushed into service in South-East Asia. It was here that the unofficial nickname 'Loach' came into use. It was a variation of the LOH acronym. Its primary role during the Vietnam War was as aerial scout for Huey gunships and Huey Cobra attack helicopters. This was an extremely dangerous job and a total of 842 were lost. Post-Vietnam War, the US Army's remaining inventory of Cayuse helicopters was transferred to the US Army National Guard.

Kiowa

The US Army reopened the LOH competition in 1967. Having its original LOH submission rejected, Bell submitted a redesigned model. As no other firms resubmitted their designs, Bell won the second round of the LOH competition by default with its

M206A helicopter named the 'Jet Ranger'. Their two-man helicopter would be designated by the US Army as the OH-58A and assigned the official nickname 'Kiowa'.

The first production units of the OH-58A Kiowa came off the assembly line in 1969 and were quickly dispatched to South-East Asia the same year. By the time American military participation in the Vietnam War concluded in 1973, a total of forty-five units had been lost. Retained in front-line service by the US Army following the Vietnam War, the OH-58A was eventually replaced by the upgraded OH-58C model fitted with a more powerful engine.

Comanche

In 1982, the US Army decided it wanted a new state-of-the-art stealth observation helicopter and invited bids for the design. This was intended to replace the 'A' and 'C' models of the OH-58 Kiowa and OH-6A Cayuse observation helicopters. The winning contender in 1991 was the team of Boeing-Sikorsky. Their proposed helicopter design was assigned the designation RAH-66 by the US Army and officially nicknamed the 'Comanche'.

The first flight of a Comanche prototype took place in 1996. Powered by two 1,563hp engines coupled together, the prototypes reached a maximum speed of 201mph. To maintain its stealth ability, all the helicopter's weapons were to be carried inside the fuselage. Sadly, like the state-of-the-art Cheyenne, the ever-increasing costs of the Comanche and a number of other factors resulted in its cancellation in 2004.

Kiowa Warrior

The final model of the Kiowa series was the OH-58D, which entered into operational service with the US Army in 1984. It was readily identifiable from the earlier 'A' and 'C' versions of the Kiowa by its beach-ball-shaped Mast Mounted Sight (MMS) affixed over the top of its rotor assembly. Within the MMS were a number of devices: a thermal imaging sight, a low-light television camera, a laser range-finder and a laser designator for illuminating targets.

Originally envisioned as being unarmed, the OH-58D was eventually fitted with external hard points on either side of its fuselage for attaching a variety of weapons. In this weapon-armed configuration the OH-58D was assigned the name 'Kiowa Warrior'. An upgraded 'F' model was planned but cancelled in 2014. The entire OH-58D Kiowa Warrior inventory was retired from US Army service in 2016 as a cost-saving measure, with its role taken over by the Apache attack helicopter working with UAVs.

Little Birds

In 1980, twenty-two units of the Cayuse were transferred from the US Army National Guard to a new US Army unit that would eventually evolve into the 160th Special

Operations Aviation Regiment, which is typically shortened to 160th SOAR. This unit is also popularly referred to as the 'Night Stalkers', with reference to its primary role of supporting US Army Special Operation Forces (SOF). The OH-64A was turned into a light attack helicopter by the 160th SOAR and received the new designation AH-6C.

Because the 160th SOAR required additional units of the Cayuse and the existing inventory had been exhausted, the US Army bought seventeen units of a commercial version of the Cayuse in 1981 known as the Hughes 500MD. With the 160th SOAR, these helicopters were designated the MH-6E and unofficially nicknamed the 'Little Birds' (as was the earlier AH-6C).

In the intervening decades the 160th SOAR has taken into service the latest models of the original Hughes 500MD design, which are designated the Model 530MG and built by Boeing. This has resulted in a series of designations that has culminated with the AH/MH-6M model – also referred to as the 'Enhanced Little Bird' – that can serve in the transport/utility role as well as the attack role due to a more powerful engine than mounted in earlier models of the helicopter.

160th SOAR Black Hawks

With its inception in 1980, what eventually became the 160th SOAR took into service thirty brand-new UH-60A Black Hawk transport helicopters. These were soon modified with more advanced avionics and, by 1984, a Forward-Looking Infra-red (FLIR) system. In 1985, sixteen of the 160th SOAR Black Hawks were fitted with a new Cockpit Management System (CMS) to reduce the pilot's workload. This resulted in the new designation MH-60A.

In 1989, the 160th SOAR acquired the UH-60L Black Hawks that were then modified with the CMS, global positioning system (GPS) and other features such as an external rescue hoist. Reflecting these add-on features, they became the MH-60L. That same year a few of the MH-60L Black Hawks were configured solely as gunships and named the Direct Action Penetrator (DAP). The latest non-classified model Black Hawk in use by the 160th SOAR is designated the MH-60M.

160th SOAR Chinooks

The Chinook series has been modified in small numbers to see service with the 160th SOAR. The first twelve were unmodified CH-47Cs acquired in 1980, which initially served only as flying fuel trucks. Eventually they were modified so they could be flown during the hours of darkness with night-vision goggles. Other features added included long-range navigation and communication equipment and external fuel tanks.

Between 1983 and 1987, twenty-seven units of the CH-47D went through a series of progressive upgrades to enhance their operational capabilities. These included such features as embedded global positioning system/inertial navigation and new engines. The various modifications resulted in the CH-47D becoming the MH-47D.

The MH-47D was followed into service with the 160th SOAR in 1994 by twenty-six units of a Chinook labelled the M-47E. It was a highly-modified model of the standard US Army CH-47C. The latest model of the Chinook to enter the specialized inventory of the 160th SOAR is the MH-47G. It has a Fast Rope Insertion & Extraction System (FRIES) and a defensive armament system consisting of three 7.62mm machine guns, two of them being mini-guns.

Pictured is a US Navy SH-2F Seasprite. It was a twin-engine helicopter optimized for the anti-submarine role (ASW). To destroy enemy submarines which it located, the helicopter was armed with depth-charges and torpedoes. Due to its compact size the SH-2F could be operated from US Navy warships other than aircraft carriers. The unofficial nickname for the 'F' model of the Seasprite was the 'Sea Pig'. (DOD)

(**Opposite, above**) The SH-2F Seasprite shown here was 54ft 7in in length and had a height of 15ft 6in. Empty it weighed 7,040lb and had a maximum take-off weight of 12,800lb. Top speed of the helicopter was 165mph with a cruising speed of 150mph. The aircraft's service ceiling was 22,500ft with an operational range of 422 miles. (*DOD*)

(**Opposite, below**) Landing a helicopter of any size on a small platform at the rear of a non-aircraft carrier can be extremely difficult, as can be attested to in this photograph of an SH-2G model of the Seasprite. The circular radome underneath the helicopter's front fuselage contained a search radar for identifying and tracking boats and ships that could then be engaged by US Navy surface ships. (*DOD*)

(**Above**) The SH-3 Sea King series helicopter first entered the US Navy inventory in 1961. The twin-engine aircraft was designed with a watertight boat-like bottom fuselage as can be discerned in this photograph to allow them to land and float in mild sea conditions. In the front wheel storage compartments were inflatable flotation bags. Above the right-hand-side fuselage door is a rescue hoist. (*DOD*)

(**Opposite, above**) The SH-3 Sea King series helicopter shown here during a training exercise had an overall length of 72ft 8in and a height of 16ft 9in. Empty they weighed 9,762lb and had a maximum take-off weight of 21,000lb. Top speed was 166mph with a range of 621 miles. They had a service ceiling of 14,700ft. In the transport role the fuselage could accommodate up to twenty-eight passengers. (*DOD*)

(**Opposite, below**) The US Navy replacement for the SH-2 Seasprite and SH-3 Sea King series helicopters in the anti-submarine (ASW) role was the SH-60B Seahawk seen here. The circular radome below the front fuselage contained the AN/APS-124 search radar unit for identifying and tracking surface vessels. The yellow and red device with the black nose, attached to a pylon at the rear of the fuselage, is the AN/ASQ-81 (V)2 Magnetic Anomaly Detector (MAD), also referred to as a dipping sonar. (*DOD*)

(**Above**) An identifying feature of the SH-60B was the two flat panel electronic support measure (ESM) blisters seen here on either side of the lower fuselage nose of the aircraft pictured. The ESM blisters are tactical electronic gathering devices for threat recognition. Mounted on the gimbal at the front of the fuselage nose is the AAQ-16 FLIR pod. (*DOD*)

(**Above**) The SH-60B Seahawk, derived from the US Army UH-60A, required extensive design changes to adapt it for the anti-submarine role. The cargo cabin door on the left-hand side of the SH-60B Seahawk was deleted, as seen here, and replaced by a window and a stub wing. Behind the stub wing is a twenty-five-round pneumatic sonobuoy launcher. (*DOD*)

(**Opposite, above**) A flight crewman of an SH-60B Seahawk poses with a sonobuoy, which would be ejected from the twenty-five-tube pneumatic launcher next to him. The sonobuoys are expendable and self-activate upon entering the water. Once in the water some versions transmit acoustic information on the presence of a submarine to a sensor operator in the helicopter. (*DOD*)

(**Opposite, below**) In the cabin of the SH-60B Seahawk is an enlisted Sensor Operator (SO). Upon locating an enemy submarine the SO could launch one of two acoustically-homing Mk 48 or Mk 50 torpedoes. The Mk 48 weighed 508lb and had a range of 12,000 yards. It has an approximately 100lb warhead and could reach a depth of 1,200ft. The Mk 50 was the replacement for the Mk 48 and entered service in 1992. (*DOD*)

(**Above**) In this picture an AGM-119 Penguin anti-ship missile has just been launched from an SH-60B Seahawk. The missile was first acquired by the US Navy in 1972. To reduce the SH-60B's footprint, allowing a small landing surface, the rear tail-wheel was 13ft forward under the tail boom compared to that of the US Army UH-60A Black Hawk. (*DOD*)

(**Opposite, above**) The SH-60F Oceanhawk pictured here is the base model of the more sophisticated, and therefore more costly, SH-60B Seahawk. It lacks the under-fuselage APS-124 search radar radome and AAQ-16 FLIR pod of the SH-60B. It has a six-tube pneumatic sonobuoy launcher and is equipped with the AQS-13 dipping sonar. (*DOD*)

(**Opposite, below**) A variant of the SH-60F Rescue Hawk is the HH-60F pictured here. Like the SH-60B Seahawk it is fitted with an AAQ-16 FLIR pod on a gimbal attached to the fuselage nose of the aircraft. Besides its role as a SAR/CSAR helicopter it can be armed with a variety of machine guns for special operation missions. (*DOD*)

(**Opposite, above**) Pictured is the MH-60R Seahawk that looks almost identical to the SH-60B. A small identifying feature of the MH-60R is the different configuration of the two flat panel electronic support measure (ESM) blisters on either side of the lower fuselage nose. Another small external difference is that the twenty-five-tube pneumatic launcher protrudes from the left-hand-side fuselage of the aircraft. (*DOD*)

(**Above**) As with all helicopters intended for shipboard deployment, the MH-60R Seahawk has been designed with a number of fold-up features as seen in this picture to reduce its storage footprint. On this particular helicopter the twenty-five-tube pneumatic launcher has been covered by a panel. The MH-60R has an integrated self-defence system like the newest generation of US Army UH-60 series Black Hawks. (*DOD*)

(**Opposite, below**) Based on the US Army UH-60L Black Hawk is the MH-60S Seahawk seen here. Note the tail wheel has not been moved forward under the tail boom as with other Seahawk models. This particular MH-60S is missing the AAQ-16 FLIR pod on its front fuselage gimbal. The small two-piece sliding window behind the cockpit is a feature of all US Army UH-60 Black Hawks. (*Christophe Vallier*)

(**Opposite, above**) Unlike all the other models of the Seahawk employed by the US Navy that had no left-hand-side cargo doors, that is not the case with the MH-60S shown in this picture. On either side of the upper fuselage nose of the aircraft can be seen the protruding AN/APR-44 radar warning receivers. It lacks the ALE-47 Chaff/Flare dispenser normally fitted to the tail boom of the MH-60R. (*DOD*)

(**Above**) The pioneering unmanned US Navy Drone Anti-Submarine Helicopter (DASH) pictured here pushed the technology of the late 1950s a bit further than that for which it was ready. It was intended to be flown from smaller US Navy warships such as destroyers and be armed with two torpedoes or a single nuclear-armed depth-charge. (*DOD*)

(**Opposite, below**) Reflecting the American military's growing interest in unmanned drones, the US Navy took into service in 2009 the MQ-8B Fire Scout helicopter seen here. It is 31ft 7in in length and 9ft 8in in height. It operates from smaller US Navy warships and provides them with a real-time intelligence-gathering platform that can also be employed in targeting. (*DOD*)

(**Opposite, above**) The operational success of the MQ-8B Fire Scout helicopter led to the US Navy taking into service a larger version seen here, designated the MQ-8C Fire Scout. As with the earlier version of the unmanned drone the 'C' model of the Fire Scout is based on a commercial helicopter design, in this case the Bell 407 Jet Ranger. (*DOD*)

(**Opposite, below**) The US Navy pioneered the concept of employing helicopters in what is referred to as the Airborne Mine Countermeasures (AMCM) role. The US Navy reconfigured nine of its SH-3A Sea King helicopters as aerial minesweepers and labelled them the RH-3A. With the advent of the much larger and more capable CH-53 Sea Stallion in 1966, the navy created AMCM variants and came up with the RH-53A and the RH-53D. An example of the latter is pictured here. (*DOD*)

(**Above**) Looking for a more powerful helicopter, the US Navy decided that the CH-53E Super Stallion, introduced into service in 1981, would be the perfect platform for a next-generation AMCM helicopter. After some redesigning the US Navy took delivery of the first units in 1986 and designated them the MH-53E Sea Dragon, an example of which is seen here. (*DOD*)

(**Above**) The biggest external difference between the CH-53E Super Stallion and the MH-53E Sea Dragon is the large sponsons on either side of the fuselage as seen here on the latter. There are various methods employed by the Sea Dragon to clear mines. Three involve towing a device of some sort through the water behind the aircraft to detonate the mines by various methods. (*DOD*)

(**Opposite, above**) Pictured is the Mk-105 minesweeping sled. It is connected to the MH-53E Sea Dragon by a 450ft cable that powers a gas turbine engine on the sled. The gas turbine engine provides electrical current to the Y-shaped arms seen on the sled that rotate in the water. They in turn simulate the magnetic or acoustic signature of a ship, causing mines to detonate. (*DOD*)

(**Opposite, below**) The MH-53E Sea Dragon can clear an area of mines by towing the AN/SPU-1W magnetized pipe seen here, either singly or three at a time. The device detonates mines by magnetic influence. Another method involves the helicopter towing through the water a steel cable with cutters that will slice through the mines' underwater mooring cables. The underwater mines will then float to the surface to be destroyed by gunfire. (*DOD*)

(**Opposite, above**) Being towed into the hangar bay of a US Navy warship is this MH-53E Sea Dragon. It is 99ft 1in in length and 28ft 4in in height. Empty it weighs 36,745lb and has a maximum take-off weight of 69,000lb. Its three engines give it a top speed of 173mph and a service ceiling of 10,000ft. On its internal fuel tanks it has a range of 1,200 miles. (*DOD*)

(**Opposite, below**) The Kaman K-600 with its single piston engine that powered two intermeshed rotor blades was adopted by the US Navy, USMC and the USAF in the 1960s for a number of different roles. The firm pushed ahead with the development of a gas turbine engine-powered version. This resulted in the USAF purchasing 193 units of the version pictured here that was designated the H-43B Huskie. (*DOD*)

(**Above**) In USAF service the primary role of the H-43B Huskie was in airfield crash and rescue work as seen in this dramatic picture of a training exercise. For this role the helicopter carried a 63-gallon container of fire-fighting foam that it would lay down near a crash site and then disembark two firefighters. The rotor wash of the helicopter could also be employed to deflect flames away from a downed aircraft. (*DOD*)

For employment as a cargo helicopter the USAF took into service 133 units of an aircraft designated the CH-3C in the early 1960s. During the Vietnam War a small number of the CH-3C helicopters were painted black as seen here on this museum aircraft and employed in a variety of covert operations throughout South-East Asia. *(USAF Museum)*

At a certain point the USAF decided that the CH-3C would make a suitable CSAR helicopter. This resulted in the HH-3E nicknamed the 'Super Jolly Green Giant' seen here during the Vietnam War. It was fitted with armour protection around key areas of the aircraft and was typically armed with at least three machine guns to provide suppressive fire during rescue missions. *(DOD)*

In this picture we see a USAF A-1 Skyraider escorting an HH-3E Super Jolly Green Giant on a CSAR mission during the Vietnam War. This programme began in 1965 as enemy anti-aircraft defences improved. Once in a search area the Skyraiders would attack enemy ground positions so the Super Jolly Green Giants could land to recover the flight crews of downed aircraft. (*USAF Museum*)

The HH-3E was the first American military helicopter to be configured for mid-air refuelling as seen here in this Vietnam War-era photograph. The helicopter would continue in the CSAR role all the way through to Operation DESERT STORM in 1991. By this time some labelled it the MH-3E, with others referring to it by the unofficial nickname of the 'Pave Pig'. (*DOD*)

(**Above**) Beginning in 1967 the USAF began replacing its HH-3E Jolly Green Giant helicopters with the Super Jolly Green Giants, an example of which is seen here. This is one of the original HH-53B models that can be identified by the two large support struts extending from the upper fuselage side to the horizontal sponson. There would be an identical arrangement on the other side of the aircraft. (*DOD*)

(**Opposite, above**) The second model in the HH-53 series was the 'C' model seen here taking part in a training exercise. It first arrived in South-East Asia in 1969. A recognition feature of the HH-53C model is that it lacks the two large support struts extending out from the upper fuselage sides of the helicopter to the horizontal sponsons as appeared on the HH-53B model. (*DOD*)

(**Opposite, below**) Pictured during a rescue mission in South-East Asia is a USAF HH-53C Super Jolly Green Giant. Unfortunately, like its predecessor, the HH-53 series helicopters were daytime and fair-weather aircraft. Near the end of America's military involvement in the Vietnam War a few of the HH-53C units were fitted with a night-vision system and took part in a small number of nighttime rescues. (*USAF Museum*)

Whereas the HH-3E Jolly Green Giant on occasion was armed with two 7.62mm machine guns, weight permitting, the HH-53 Super Jolly Green Giant series helicopters were much more powerful and could be armed with up to three of the GAU-2B/A mini-guns, one of which is seen here in use during the war in South-East Asia. *(DOD)*

On display is the MH-53M Pave Low IV. Its last service flight took place in Iraq on 28 March 2008. Prior to that occasion it saw service during both Operation DESERT STORM in 1991 and Operation IRAQI FREEDOM in 2003. On the front lower fuselage can be seen the large number of radomes that contained the sensors employed to fly the helicopter at night and in adverse weather conditions. *(USAF Museum)*

Included among the sensor arrays mounted on the front fuselage of the MH-53 Pave Low series helicopter pictured would be FLIR and terrain-following radar. Other sensors carried on board would be the Global Positioning System (GPS) and an Inertial Navigation System (INS). The aircraft carried a crew of six: two pilots, two flight engineers and two gunners. *(DOD)*

(**Above**) Taking part in a training exercise is an MH-53J Pave Low III. The helicopter had a length of 88ft and a height of 17ft 2in. Empty it weighed 23,570lb and had a maximum take-off weight of 42,000lb. The maximum speed was 196mph with a service ceiling of 16,000ft. Its range on external fuel tanks was 540 miles. (*DOD*)

(**Opposite, above**) In this picture an MH-63M Pave Low IV is attempting a refuelling hook-up. We can also see the rescue hoist just above the right-hand-side cabin door. The two gunners on the aircraft could, depending on the mission requirements, be armed with two or more 7.62mm GAU-2B/A mini-guns or larger 12.7mm (.50 calibre) machine guns. In the transport role the helicopter could carry as many as thirty-eight passengers. (*DOD*)

(**Opposite, below**) The CV-22B Osprey is the much more advanced USAF Special Operations Command (AFSOC) version of the MV-22B used by the USMC. Like the MH-63M Pave Low IV which it replaced, the CV-22B is fitted with an array of lower front fuselage radomes as seen in this picture. These house the various sensors that allow it to fly in conditions that would ground the USMC version of the Osprey. (*DOD*)

(**Opposite, above**) The cockpit of the USAF CV-22B Osprey, like all modern American military helicopters, has a digital multi-function instrument panel commonly referred to as a 'glass cockpit'. The first example of the CV-22B was delivered to the USAF in 2007. Initial operational status was achieved in 2009. The last of the fifty-one units of the CV-22B are to be delivered to the USAF by 2019. (*DOD*)

(**Opposite, below**) In the foreground of this picture we see a single USAF HH-60G Pave Hawk. Behind it are two MH-60 series Pave Low helicopters. The primary mission of the Pave Hawk is CSAR/SAR for which it is equipped with a personnel-locating system that provides range and bearing information for a survivor using a PRC-112 military-issue survival radio. (*DOD*)

(**Above**) Besides the military CSAR/SAR roles, the USAF HH-60G Pave Hawk seen here has also been tasked with a wide range of non-military roles. These have included over its time in service the medical evacuation of civilians and various types of humanitarian assistance during disasters. To perform these many roles it has a hoist capable of lifting 600lb. (*DOD*)

(**Opposite, above**) In the early 1960s, the US Army took into service the first of approximately 100 units of the CH-54 Tarhe seen here. The bare-bones appearance of the aircraft reflected in the lack of even engine cowlings was the US Army's way of saving weight. Empty, the aircraft weighed 19,800lb with a maximum take-off weight of 47,000lb. (*Paul and Loren Hannah*)

(**Above**) The CH-54 Tarhe had a length of 88ft 6in and a height of 25ft 5in. The Universal Military Pod (UMP) pictured could carry as many as eighty-seven passengers or be configured as a command and control centre or a mobile field hospital. Empty, the helicopter weighed 19,800lb and had a maximum take-off weight of 47,000lb. Its top speed was 150mph and range 230 miles. (*DOD*)

(**Opposite, below**) Pictured is a restored OH-6A Cayuse observation helicopter, better known to those who flew it during the Vietnam War as the 'Loach'. In South-East Asia it typically worked in conjunction with either US Army Huey gunships or AH-1 Huey Cobra attack helicopters by identifying targets for them to engage. Depending on the crew's preference it could be either armed or unarmed. (*Paul and Loren Hannah*)

(**Above**) In this US Army museum Vietnam War diorama we see a downed UH-1 Iroquois/Huey in the foreground and overhead an OH-6A Cayuse/Loach. The OH-6A first arrived in South-East Asia in 1967. The helicopter had a length of 26ft 4in and a height of 8ft 2in. Empty it weighed 1,229lb with a maximum take-off weight of 2,400lb. Top speed was 150mph. (*Paul and Loren Hannah*)

(**Opposite, above**) Despite the high regard in which those who flew the OH-6A Cayuse/Loach during the Vietnam War held the helicopter, that feeling was not shared by the US Army's senior leadership, who felt that Hughes had been too difficult to deal with and sought an alternative observation helicopter design. That helicopter, seen here, was the Bell OH-58, named the 'Kiowa'. (*DOD*)

(**Opposite, below**) On museum display is an OH-58 Kiowa-series helicopter, which first reached South-East Asia in 1969 as the intended replacement for the OH-6A Cayuse/Loach. The version of the Kiowa that saw service during the Vietnam War was designated the OH-58A. Post-Vietnam War an upgraded model with a more powerful engine, labelled the OH-58C, took the place of the earlier version. (*Paul and Loren Hannah*)

(**Above**) Parked are a number of commercial versions of the original OH-58 series Kiowa helicopter that are employed by the US Navy as training aircraft. In this role they are designated the TH-57 Sea Ranger and have dual flight controls. They are also employed to train USMC helicopter pilots. In US Army service as a training aircraft it is referred to as the TH-67 Creek. (*DOD*)

(**Opposite, above**) In this photograph we see one of the two RAH-66 Comanche prototypes. The helicopter was designed to be an extremely stealthy aerial observation platform with all its weapons carried internally, including a retractable three-barrel 20mm cannon. The original plans called for initial delivery to the US Army to begin in 2006; however, it was cancelled by the army in 2004. (*DOD*)

(**Opposite, below**) With the cancellation of the RAH-66 Comanche, the US Army was forced to rethink what it needed in a state-of-the-art observation helicopter that was at the same time affordable. The answer was the OH-58D that when armed became the OH-58D Kiowa Warrior pictured here. The most noticeable external feature of the aircraft was its Mast-Mounted Sight (MMS). (*DOD*)

(**Opposite, above**) In this picture we see two US Army OH-58D Kiowa Warriors prepared to go on patrol over Iraq during America's long occupation of that country. Both are armed with a single M296 12.7mm (.50 calibre) machine gun on the left-hand side of their fuselage. The gun is fed from a semi-external magazine carrying 500 rounds of ammunition. (*DOD*)

(**Opposite, below**) Inside the cockpit of a US Army OH-58D Kiowa Warrior flying over Afghanistan we can see the M9 semi-automatic pistol strapped to the pilot's chest and the smoke-marking grenades on the top of the instrument panel. The helicopter is 42ft 2in in length and has a height of 12ft 11in. Its top speed is 147mph with a service ceiling of 15,000ft. (*DOD*)

(**Above**) In 2011, the US Army announced plans for the newest version of the OH-58 series to be designated the OH-58F Kiowa Warrior. Rather than the Mast-Mounted Sight (MMS) of the 'D' model, its electronic sensors would be mounted under the lower front fuselage as is seen in this photograph of a prototype. The programme was cancelled in 2014 and the US Army's inventory of the OH-58D Kiowa Warriors was pulled from service in 2016. (*DOD*)

The forming in the early 1980s of what eventually became the 160th Special Operations Aviation Regiment (160th SOAR) resulted in a small number of Vietnam War vintage OH-6A Cayuse helicopters being placed back into service as the MH-6E troop transport. Their current replacement, seen here, is the commercial version of the helicopter labelled the Model 530F, which the US Army designates the MH-6M. (*DOD*)

(**Opposite, above**) Pictured here is an MH-6M series transport helicopter belonging to the 160th SOAR. Visible are the two fuselage side passenger platforms, each of which can seat three people. The popular nickname for the 160th SOAR is the 'Night Stalkers'. The MH-6 series helicopters are popularly referred to as 'Little Birds'. Those based on the Model 530F are called 'Enhanced Little Birds'. (*DOD*)

(**Opposite, below**) Preparing for take-off are two AH-60M Enhanced Little Bird gunships. Note that unlike the MH-6M transport helicopter version, the AH-6M gunship model has a FLIR system mounted under the front of the fuselage on a gimbal. Both aircraft are armed with a single three-barrel 30mm M230 Chain Gun. (*DOD*)

In the foreground of this picture is an MH-60M Black Hawk and in the background an MH-47G Chinook. Both belong to the 160th SOAR. Based on experience gained in Afghanistan it was found that the MH-47G Chinook when employed in the air assault troop transport role rather than merely as a logistical platform could replace up to five of the MH-60M Black Hawks. *(DOD)*